Generation 2K

What Parents & Others NEED TO KNOW About the Millennials

Wendy Murray Zoba

InterVarsity Press
Downers Grove, Illinois

InterVarsity Press
P.O. Box 1400, Downers Grove, IL 60515
World Wide Web: www ivpress.com
E-mail: mail@ivpress.com

©1999 by Wendy Murray Zoba

InterVarsity Press® is the book-publishing division of InterVarsity Christian Fellowship/USA®, a student movement active on campus at hundreds of universities, colleges and schools of nursing in the United States of America, and a member movement of the International Fellowship of Evangelical Students. For information about local and regional activities, write Public Relations Dept., InterVarsity Christian Fellowship/USA, 6400 Schroeder Rd., P.O. Box 7895, Madison, WI 53707-7895.

Scripture quotations are taken from the Holy Bible, New Living Translation, *copyright © 1996. Used by permission of Tyndale House Publishers, Inc., Wheaton, Illinois 60189, U.S.A. All rights reserved.*

Cover photograph: SuperStock

ISBN 0-8308-2211-9

Printed in the United States of America ♻

Library of Congress Cataloging-in-Publication Data

Zoba, Wendy Murray.
   Generation 2K : what parents and others need to know about the
millennials / Wendy Murray Zoba.
     p.   cm.
   Includes bibliographical references.
   ISBN 0-8308-2211-9 (alk. paper)
   1 Parent and teenager.   I. Title.
HQ799.15.Z62   1999
306.874—dc21

                                        99-15059
                                           CIP

15 14 13 12 11 10 9 8 7 6 5 4 3 2

11 10 09 08 07 06 05 04 03 02 01 00 99

*To my father
Myles N. Murray
in memoriam*

Contents

Acknowledgments

I would like to acknowledge the following people who have been instrumental in enabling me to complete this project.

I appreciate the helpfulness of and input from Ed and Cathi Basler, Greg and Susan Jones, and John Ruhlman, who spearheaded and implemented the church models I highlight in chapter five. I also would like to thank Steve Andres, youth pastor at Calvary Church in Naperville, Illinois, and members of his youth group who participated in the survey I took in the summer of 1997, portions of which also appear in chapter five.

Romane Phillips, Vanessa Owens, James Seward, Tony Sok, Donny Vega and Mary Wilson each contributed cogent and sometimes surprising elements to the "teen forum on the church" I sponsored in May 1998. Their authenticity, commitment, tenacity and wisdom beyond their years inspired me. Their stories and discussion are found in chapters two and six of the book. Thanks to *Christianity Today* for enabling me to sponsor this forum.

I am grateful to my colleagues John Wilson, for persisting in his recommendation to do this book; and Carla Sonheim, who has been a sounding board and helpful friend. I am especially indebted to Mickey Maudlin, who advised me and worked with me at many stages of this project. Cindy Bunch-Hotaling at InterVarsity Press has been an excellent editor and has helped me to see my weak spots. I shudder to think where I would be without good editors.

I have many dear friends who have prayed me through this. Karen Maudlin and Wendy Wilson have been especially vigilant.

My three sons, Nate, Ben and Jon (and their many friends), have filled our lives with a lot of laughter and spontaneous wrestling bouts (and some broken furniture). They have been a continual education in the world according to teens and have kept me on the cutting edge of the teen issues. My beloved husband, Bob, in turn, has steadied me when the cutting edge has become the jagged edge.

I am grateful to the Lord, who has heard my prayers and who continues to hear them.

1

The Stakes

Bucky, Moon and Boop Murray were looking for entertainment, such as could be found in Liverpool, Pennsylvania—population six hundred—during the Depression, so they tipped an outhouse. They never knew who the poor soul was who was using it at the time. They were in too big a hurry to evade the law—that is, Dilly Stailey, the town constable. They knew Dilly was afraid to go into the cemetery on the hill that overlooked the town, so they ran there.

There wasn't much to do in that small canal town on the west bank of the Susquehanna River in the 1930s, but Bucky, Moon and Boop, along with Mullet Mouth Stailey, Weezy Long, Puggy Deckard and Hambone Dodge, managed to keep themselves entertained. (The nicknames got started as a result of some "personal embarrassment of the unfortunate person," said Moon.) On Shrove Tuesday (the day before Ash Wednesday) they locked the schoolhouse door so the teacher couldn't get in, for which Moon Murray received the principal's version of corporal punishment, "which I deserved," he said. On another occasion they collected ripe dog droppings in a paper sack, which they placed on a neighbor's porch and set on fire, and howled with laughter from the bushes as the neighbor stamped the fire out.

Each evening in Liverpool the fire siren sounded at 8:30, signaling the beginning of curfew for everyone under sixteen. But the Murray brothers, even after they turned sixteen, weren't home much later than that. "Mom didn't like to see us get out and around because of the possibility of losing her control over us," recalled Moon. ("We didn't have any place to go anyway," he said.)

Moon had gotten his nickname when he had been beaten up for being fat, resulting in two black eyes. His tormentors had told him he looked like the comic-strip character Moon Mullens who also had two black eyes, so that's why they called him Moon. The irony was Moon Murray only had one eye. He had been four years old when Billy Boals, the street bully, had hit him with a stick and blinded him. ("The last thing I remember I saw with that eye was a pillow with three roses embroidered thereon.") But Moon didn't complain about it. In fact, he credited his handicap for driving him to aspire to be "better than average."

Moon had received thirty-one merit badges in the Boy Scouts and was just one short of making Eagle Scout when one day he "looked up to the mountain and decided to get at it." He set the pace for the whole of troop 91, which along with troops 19, 24, 51, 52, 92 and 160 broke the Harrisburg Area Council's record for the largest number of scouts to attain the Eagle rank in a single year.

When Moon graduated from high school, he finished first in the state in history and eighth in the state overall. The Daughters of the American Revolution and several universities offered him full scholarships for college, but his mother, Sara Murray, talked him out of accepting them because, as he described it, "I didn't have good clothes."

Sara Murray, Moon recalled, was "mostly impressed by the punishing God," which had him panicked enough to go forward on more than one occasion when the parson issued his weekly altar call. But Moon's mother possessed a softer side, which she summoned frequently while raising her three sons. Each year for Moon's birthday she made him his favorite devil's food cake from scratch with sour milk. At Christmas she made raisin-filled cookies and stuffed her boys' black socks with nuts, hard candy, a candy cane and an orange in the toe. On New Year's

Eve she served fried oysters and pork sauerkraut without fail.

So there were some highlights for Moon Murray in his otherwise chronically hard life growing up in Liverpool, Pennsylvania, during the Depression. Moon and the Liverpool gang enjoyed the first-edition *Superman* and *Batman* comics, listened to *The Green Hornet* and *The Shadow* on the radio, and discovered the magic of Al Jolson in *The Singing Fool* and Boris Karloff in *The Hunchback of Notre Dame* at the local movie theater. They grew up when medicine shows advertised cures for corns and calluses and the ragman went door to door buying worn-out clothes for the paper industry. They witnessed the birth of the Greyhound Bus Company when luggage was carried on top and the increase in the price of cars from three hundred to six hundred dollars. They saw the soap industry revolutionized by the onset of indoor plumbing, and they watched the iceman go the way of the outhouse when he was replaced by the Frigidaire.

> Moon and the Liverpool gang enjoyed the first-edition *Superman* and *Batman* comics, listened to *The Green Hornet* and *The Shadow* on the radio, and discovered the magic of Al Jolson in *The Singing Fool* and Boris Karloff in *The Hunchback of Notre Dame* at the local movie theater.

Changing Times

But as the voice of the baby-boom generation once rasped, "the times, they are a changin'." Bob Dylan's prophetic laments and other aspects of my world as a teen would have been unrecognizable to Bucky, Moon and Boop. Unlike the Murray brothers, whose neighborhood consisted of raised houses with double doors and wooden porches facing the riverbank and with outhouses in the back, I grew up in the newly developed Midwestern suburbs, where games of kick-the-can spanned all the manicured and sprawling lawns in the neighborhood. Our yard alone had a tetherball setup in the front and an in-ground swimming pool, two patios and a fire pit in the back. Every night during the Ohio summers of my teen years, our driveway was filled with the cars of friends who had come over for what had become nightly pool parties. We played blind tag in the deep end and listened to the Beach Boys blaring from the stereo speakers perched against my bedroom window.

School days, for me, consisted largely of the drive to school in the Fiat provided for me by my parents, after-school cheerleading practice and, once I was home, a steady dose of afternoon TV talk shows while I consumed Tab and Ho-Hos.

My father, Moon Murray, built this life of material abundance for us in his determination to reinvent himself outside the suffocating provinciality of Liverpool. He said once, "I went to Middletown Air Depot for $1,440 a year until I could get into the Army. Then it was goodbye Liverpool, poverty, family strife and stagnation." So despite his mother's attempted sabotage (Sara Murray was my grandmother, whom we called Button), his ticket out of Liverpool was the United States Army. He served in the HQ 63rd General Depot in the Aleutian Islands in a noncombat capacity (because of his one eye), intercepting the radio messages of Tokyo Rose. He made it to college too, in Ohio, where he met my mother. He never returned to Liverpool except to visit his mother and brothers, who had never left. He launched his own business, which evolved into a million-dollar success story—which explains why I had the luxury to eat Ho-Hos by the boxful and to host swimming parties on summer nights.

My affluent youth may not represent a typical baby-boomer childhood, but such extravagance was not atypical either. Susan Littwin, in her book *The Postponed Generation,* writes of the baby-boom generation (quoting *Newsweek* magazine): "Never have so many children been such complete strangers to famine, plague, want, or war. Theirs are the blessings of prosperity, theirs the spoils of peace." Littwin herself adds, "The mood of the time was so ebulliently experimental, so convinced that we [baby boomers] were entitled to the good life that somebody had at least to try the wicked notion of throwing clothes away instead of taking care of them."[1]

Leisure, prosperity and sheer numbers opened the way for the generation who had it all handed to them to emerge as revolutionaries who wanted to write their own rules. Bob Dylan proclaimed that "*every*body must get stoned," and the Beatles encouraged us to "do it in the road" (though people I knew opted for doing it under blankets at Bread concerts). We were all "okay," no matter what our proclivities, and home as the epicenter of life had begun to fragment as moms capitalized on the liberation awakened by microwave ovens and *The Feminine Mystique.* The pace of cultural transformation significantly quickened as the baby boomers came of age. The Murray brothers, who were parents of teens by that point, found it disorienting.

"Some of this was wonderful," writes Littwin, and "much of it was inevitable." However, "a lot of it was delusional. . . . It is hard to say when all the experimenting started to turn sinister."[2]

And so, it seems, the times are still changing. We who burned our bras and draft cards and celebrated the Summer of Love—we who would not trust anyone over thirty—are in our forties and fifties. We are the establishment! And we are nose to nose with the revolution we created. We see it in the faces of our teenage offspring.

Many boomers are recognizing that something has gone "off the boil" (to borrow J. I. Packer's terminology). For a long time the church has asserted a moral voice in an increasingly amoral culture, and at times it has borne the derision of more liberal-minded cultural critics. But what has been notable to me of late has been that the tone of many of these self-confessed social liberals has moved from stridency to bewilderment. There is a marked outcry from secular voices that echoes what many from within the church have been saying for decades. My research in this book highlights observations of *secular* social critics. For example, Diana West writes in the *Wall Street Journal*, "As the flower children have gone to seed, we now reap their bitter fruit."[3] Evan Thomas, in *Newsweek*, writes, "Somehow letting it all hang out did not bring freedom, just child-support payments, and the sexual revolution bequeathed us AIDS and date rape."[4] And exploring why one teen would murder another teen, Randall Sullivan, in

Rolling Stone, writes, "Did somebody out there believe these kids were watching *Pulp Fiction* 10, 15, 20 times to be instructed or uplifted?"[5]

These comments reflect the larger testimony that is emerging from many sectors of today's society. Whether it is in the realm of politics, entertainment, education or religion, people of all ages and dispositions are nonplused about some of today's social signals. It is evident that American society as a whole is reaching the point where it is looking for answers.

This is a moment of opportunity for the church. Some aspects of today's culture are so shocking and dismaying that some within the believing community might be tempted to retreat, hunker down and let society go to hell, with the hope of accelerating the Lord's return. This is the approach that the fundamentalists of the early 1900s adopted. I understand that temptation.

But to shrink back from cultural engagement, regardless of its banalities and effrontery, would be an abdication of our missiological mandate to go into "all the world" as Jesus instructed. He was the master of meeting people on their terms and on their turf. If we are to have a voice and be effective transmitters of a relevant gospel to the next generations, we will have to follow his lead. We might not like where that takes us—perhaps to the mosh pit or the tattoo parlor—but if today's youth are going to be reached, those of us who bear the weight of that mandate need to recognize that they are a different breed. They are confronting and assimilating social circumstances and forces that have never before tested the human spirit.

Their environment has affected their worldview. Their worldview informs their understanding of God. That understanding can be either validated or nullified by the church. It is time to ask whether our churches, in whatever tradition or ministry style, are empowering or inhibiting young people in their search for the face of God.

It is a delicate dance. And even when we have the best of intentions it is extremely difficult to know how far to go in engaging the culture or when to retreat.

Generational Disorientation

Sullivan, in the *Rolling Stone* article, says that today's teens are facing "generational disorientation."[6] This disorientation and its effects are especially acute for teens and their parents who happen to be Christian. A professor of mine at seminary once said that as Christians wrestle with the encroachment of a culture that is markedly hostile to evangeli-

> It is time to ask whether our churches, in whatever tradition or ministry style, are empowering or inhibiting young people in their search for the face of God.

cal sensibilities, it is more dangerous to isolate our kids than it is to expose them to it in small doses—like an inoculation. Give them enough of it to rally their spiritual antibodies, he said, stretching the metaphor, but not enough to cause them to succumb. That sounds reasonable enough, but the question that confronts parents, educators, church leaders and me is: in this environment of cultural forces, many of which defy Christian convictions, how much is "a little"?

This dilemma confronted me in the summer of 1996 when my then-sixteen-year-old son asked, "Can I go to Lollapalooza?"

"Lolla-what?" I asked.

"You know—Lollapa*looza*. The *rock* concert. It's been around forever—probably even when you were a kid."

Actually it was 1991 when the summer concert tour of several noted alternative bands began its all-day nihilistic hoedowns—"Woodstock for the piercing set"[7]—in major cities throughout the United States.

I, in characteristic nonresponse, told him I'd think about it, which I did. And every thought centered on why my answer had to be "Absolutely not." The concert, I read somewhere, exploited teen rebellion by glorifying confrontation, was predicated on sensuality and was best interpreted when one was under the influence of alcohol.

This precipitated a crisis for me. At what point, I asked myself, do I relinquish my role as the gatekeeper of my son's moral and spiritual choices? At what point do I surrender him to the forces of the youth culture that woo—dare I say pummel—him? Would my allowing him to go to Lollapalooza "inoculate" him—or subjugate him?

Like good Christian parents, my husband and I had zealously guarded our sons' God-centered upbringing. As preschoolers they rehearsed the Bible verses I wrote out for them in colored markers and for which I configured arm motions to invigorate the memorization process. They liked that. I got good at it.

I scoured Christian bookstores for versions of children's devotional books and Bibles, which we read, sometimes reread, religiously. I sang "Jesus Loves Me" as they laid their heads on their pillows at night. They grew up with no illusions about what Christmas means (once when my father asked our oldest son, who was four at the time, what "Santy Claus" was going to bring him for Christmas, he responded, "You can think about him and you can pretend he's real, but he's not"), and they never made a connection between the bunny myth and Resurrection Sunday. I had those poor boys learning the Greek alphabet before they could read.

They spent their preschool years in what my husband and I called the "Christian ghetto"—married student housing—at the seminary we attended. So every biblical gleaning they received from us at our dinner table or during prayers at night was reinforced by some other vigilant parent overseeing deliberations at the sandbox or the swing set.

We moved from the Christian ghetto to the glass house of the pastor's parsonage. But I can honestly say I never expected more of my boys for being a pastor's kids than I would have if they'd been a plumber's kids. They were *Christians,* and that carried its own set of expectations. They opened their hymnals and sang the verses and read the responsive readings not because their father was in the pulpit but because we were in church and this was worship and everyone participated.

We went to the mission field too. After four-plus years in the small-town church setting, we sold everything we owned (which came to about a thousand dollars) and moved to Central America, where my husband served as pastor to the expatriate community in Honduras's capital city. There the boys were exposed to begging street children, rolling power outages, food shortages, street crime, a cholera epidemic and lack of emission control standards. They chased down a street hood who had snatched one of their baseball caps (right off the head), and they daily endured a forty-minute school-bus ride up and down a mountain (with no guard rails), breathing fumes and coming home with crushing headaches and nauseated stomachs. They built concrete floors in the barrios for families with twice as many kids as we had and only one room to live in. They assisted work teams we sponsored from the United States with various projects, and they shared holiday celebrations with our many mission-minded friends who, like us, were so far from home.

So the four years we lived in Honduras during our sons' middle years (before adolescence) exposed them to both the hardship and the rewards of missionary life. The experience enlarged their worldview as well as their souls.

We returned to the United States when it was time for our oldest son to enter high school. And that is when all of those Christian tethers, so carefully woven and fastidiously guarded by me, were put to the test. I began to sense forces pulling my teenage sons into another orb.

Forces like Lollapalooza.

My dismay over the concert was exacerbated by the fact that, Lollapalooza aside, my son, at sixteen, was a lot better kid than I had been at his age. I grew up with peers who made marijuana brownies, and I had friends who shamelessly celebrated another month without an unwanted pregnancy. I personally didn't buy in to this revolution indiscriminately—I didn't get high and I never embraced sexual promiscuity. But I rallied around my friends who did. I laid claim to a new understanding of "freedom" when I brazenly wore hot pants and halter tops. I glorified the notion of vigilante idealism and individualism. Billy Jack inspired me.

So here I am, a mother who would be appalled if my sons brought home a girl wearing hot pants and who is left to watch helplessly as the world they inhabit—the world *my* generation created—assaults them and infiltrates the precious world I fashioned for them. Film critic David Denby remarks that "parents can still control some of the schedule, but a large part of it has been wrenched out of their hands by pop culture."[8] I have concluded that I would have to tie my sons to their beds and never let them see the light of day if I wanted to retain total control of their worlds. Regardless of my own vigilance in restricting my son's exposure to certain movies or TV shows, the mother of the teen down the street whom my son visits might not care, might have no clue or, more plausibly, might not be home at all—thus giving free rein to her kid and my son to view any movie or TV show they might be tempted to watch.

Sara Murray may have fretted over Rhett Butler's shocking curse word at the end of *Gone with the Wind,* and Moon Murray—my dad—was confounded by the wild popularity of a song whose lyrics included, basically, "Hello/Goodbye." I, in turn, am affronted by songs like "Prison Sex" (about homosexual rape) and lyrics like "I lie just to be real, and I'd die just to feel."[9] The culture today has ratcheted up the shock level of what can be heard in our music or seen in the movies or on television. It wouldn't be so bad if these elements reflected the depravity of a clandestine underground movement. But they do not; they are part of the mainstream media. The shock levels are accommodating what the culture wants and demands. The degradation is one thing our young people confront; the consuming mindset of culture writ large is another thing. Both of these forces must somehow be penetrated and redeemed by the church if we are to have any hope of passing the gospel torch to the next generation.

I look behind me and see the less complicated (but no less tortured) life lived by my father and his brothers in Liverpool, tipping outhouses and tormenting Dilly Stailey. I look before me and see the market-driven, overly stimulated, shocking world of my own three sons. Sara Murray and I come together on this point: I don't want my sons "to get out much" either. I want to keep them in the sphere of my dominion.

But my grandmother and I come together someplace else too. We will fail in our attempts to keep our children safe in the world we have fashioned for them. The day will come—just as it did when my father shook the dust of Liverpool off his feet—that our children will follow their own courses. Even if we succeed in navigating them through their youth, protecting them from some of the more degrading elements in today's culture, they still live and function in a society that is shaped by consumerism and that carries its own effects. With or without our permission or their conscious acquiescence, our youth *will* confront this culture. Even if they have grown up clueless about Bart Simpson, Eddie Vedder or Jackie Chan, if they are going to effectively minister and serve in their own context they will have to confront the effects of this culture in the lives of their peers.

Letting Go

We allowed our son to go to Lollapalooza. It violated every impulse in my theretofore-unchallenged role as the "music nazi." (No tape or CD passed into the ears of my children without first passing into mine. I retained veto power and exercised it.) Throughout the evening he was gone, I wrestled with my fears, my controlling nature, my attitude of trust, my hope in God. My son came home none the worse, went to bed, and wore his Lollapalooza T-shirt the rest of the summer (it pictured a smirking devil in a top hat).

> Even if they have grown up clueless about Bart Simpson, Eddie Vedder or Jackie Chan, if they are going to effectively minister and serve in their own context they will have to confront the effects of this culture in the lives of their peers.

I have a close friend who told me that on the day she relinquished her son, she pictured herself carrying him in her arms up an aisle to an altar. She laid him on the altar and, without a wince, turned around and walked away. She didn't look back. She told me, "I've been tempted, but I have never taken him back off of that altar."

I tried the same exercise in my mind. The problem was, I kept seeing myself crawling shamelessly back to the altar and yanking him off.

I found another picture that captured the moment for me. What came to my mind when I reckoned with the moment of surrendering my son to his own course—cutting the tethers with which I had so painstakingly bound him—was a picture of me standing alone at the edge of a precipice. In this picture no one is with me. I am looking out into the undefined vacuum. I have climbed this mountain with my son, and now I stand on the edge—I've come as far as I can go.

I wonder if my dear son remembers any of those Bible verses we rehearsed together with arm motions when he was little. Does he hear "Jesus Loves Me" when he puts his head on his pillow at night? I think about all the Christian schools he has attended through the years, where he gained command of the basic biblical and theological concepts. Will the "concepts" carry him through the turbulent course of his newfound release? He has sat in a church pew every Sunday of his life. He has sung the hymns and read the responsive readings.

I cast my son over the edge. (If I don't, he will jump.)

Who will catch him?

Key Points

☐ The generation that grew up during the Depression carried the effects of their culture into adulthood. They knew the value of a dollar and worked hard to ensure that their offspring didn't suffer similar deprivation.

☐ The generation that grew up during the baby boom reaped the benefits of their parents' financial well-being and self-discipline. Television was quickly evolving into a consumerist medium and baby boomers were the first generation to come of age in an electronic media environment.

☐ Leisure and prosperity handed baby boomers the luxury of social rebellion and the pursuit of individual freedoms. Their revolution changed the cultural ethos of the nation.

☐ Baby boomers today are facing the results of the world they created in the lives of their teenage offspring, and what they see scares them.

☐ The stakes have been raised in terms of what it means to be a teen in the context of today's consuming culture.

Prayer Point

Lord, help our young people as they navigate the turbulent waters of today's youth culture. Help us as their mentors to be wise and courageous.

2

Who Are
These People?

The *New York Times* recently devoted a special section to teens asking, "Who Are These People, Anyway?"[1] The section opens: "Trying to label America's nearly 60 million teenagers is about as easy as staying on the trail of a snowboarder in a whiteout." The writer then includes the following description of "teens today": "bubbly Hanson fans," "moody Marilyn Manson devotees," "marijuana-smoking homeboys," "savvy junior entrepreneurs," "bornagain virgins," "single moms," "student activists," "frustrated truants." What is notable, the writer concludes, is that "one teenager might inhabit several of those identities."[2]

Here is what some youth experts say about today's teens:

☐ They've eaten from the tree of knowledge.

☐ They process information in narrative images.

☐ They don't trust adults.

☐ Their "B.S. detectors" are always on.

☐ Their focus is fragmented.

☐ They've had everything handed to them.

☐ They are jaded.

☐ They have a "been there, done that" attitude.[3]

And here is what some of today's teens say about themselves:

☐ The word *teenager* is synonymous with, like, headache.[4]

☐ No one has any sense of honor anymore.

☐ We have no one to look up to; we have nothing stable to grasp.

☐ We worry all the time.

☐ We're just coasting.

☐ We're not standing for anything.

☐ We desperately need to be standing for something.

☐ Teens want God; they will look for him.[5]

Authors William Strauss and Neil Howe, in their book *Generations*, offer helpful tools for understanding the ebb and flow of social forces that act upon generations.[6] For the purposes of this book I have adapted the material from *Generations* that focuses on the twentieth century, especially as it relates to today's "Millennial" teens (born between 1977 and 1994).[7]

My research and exposure to today's teen culture has left me, in equal parts, scratching my head and inspired and encouraged. I can't help but be troubled by songs I hear over the radio by groups with names like Porno for Pyros, 7 Year Bitch, and the Sex Pistols. Yet I've seen kids sitting in my TV room watching a video and fast-forwarding sexual situations.

To gain a greater sense of how young people interpret their own youth culture, I invited six young people from differing social, racial and ethnic backgrounds to participate in an all-day forum to discuss their ideas about their world and the role of the church. This chapter will introduce them and allow us to hear their thoughts about the forces that are shaping them. We will meet them again in a later chapter when they discuss their understanding of the church.[8]

All of the teens who participated in the forum shared the commonalities of having a living relationship with the Lord Jesus, participating actively in church life and possessing an intimate knowledge of youth culture.

Tony (seventeen) immigrated to the United States from Cambodia at the age of two and "turned a Christian" when he was six. He attends a nondenominational church and has participated in an accountability group at his youth group. He recently joined the army to help pay for college. He likes the music of Five Iron Frenzy and watches *Fresh Prince* on TV. Tony did not watch the last episode of *Seinfeld.* ("My cable broke.")

Vanessa (seventeen) attends an African-American Baptist church and "accepted the Lord" at the age of eight. She has served as the president of the Teens Living for Christ youth program at her church and as the secretary of the church choir. Basically, she says, she's "just really active" at church. Her favorite television show is *7th Heaven,* and she did not watch the last episode of *Seinfeld.* ("When was it?")

James (eighteen), a SWM (single white male), was "born into a God-fearing family," was "raised in strong churches" and "said the prayer" when he was four. He graduated from high school in 1998, attends the University of Chicago and is part of a church-plant in the community of Hyde Park. He has been active in his youth group and led a Bible study at his high school. He loves the music of Supertones and Sixpence None the Richer and did not see the final episode of *Seinfeld.* ("I have no TV.")

Dionicio ("Donny," fifteen), a Mexican-American, grew up in a Christian family and, as he put it, "accepted Christ ever since I was, like, two years old." He went through a period of rebellion "because of too much TV," but found his way back to a living faith after his family "finally got channel 36" (a Christian station). Bones-Thugs-n-Harmony is one of his favorite musical groups, and his favorite television show is *The Box.* Donny did not watch the last episode of *Seinfeld.*

Mary (seventeen), a SWF, grew up in a Christian family and accepted Christ when she was five. Since then she has "just always been excited about church and youth group." When her church was searching for a new pastor she became very involved "in a lot of committees and stuff, helping with other services because they needed people to pitch in." She loves the "deep faith" and "searching lyrics" of the musical group Jars of Clay, and she was too busy to watch the last episode of *Seinfeld.* ("I had a small-group meeting at church.")

Romane (eighteen), an African-American, grew up in the inner city (he witnessed—and almost fell victim to—a drive-by shooting), and became a Christian at a Christian camp at the age of eight. He lived with his single mom until the age of fourteen, when he moved out of the city to spend his high-school years living with his grandparents. (His grandmother gets him up for church every Sunday morning, regardless of what time he gets in on Saturday night.) He graduated from high school in 1998 and attends the University of Iowa on an athletic scholarship. He listens to the music of Puff Daddy, Notorious Big, Master P and Big Puncher, and his favorite show is *Seinfeld.* He did watch the last episode, but says "it was the worst one." ("They tried too hard. It upset me.")

When Kids Kill Kids

To launch our discussion we talked about the shocking series of schoolyard killings that took place in 1997 and 1998 when young people opened fire on their peers. (Though the massacre at Columbine High School in Little-ton, Colorado, hadn't occurred at the time of the forum, the issues brought to bear in this discussion pertain in equal measure to the circumstances surrounding this tragedy.) "What is happening?" I asked.

Donny said, "My weak-minded friends will listen to Tupac or Notorious and start hearing something about killing someone or running from the law and they'll apply it to their lives. They'll eventually end up killing someone and running from the cops." He said that weak-minded people who listen to music and watch TV won't be able to "differentiate between the right and wrong in it."

Romane disagreed. He has been watching "violent stuff" since he "can remember," he said. "I've seen R-rated movies. I've seen gangs. I've seen drugs. You got to figure out what kind of person you are. You can be changed if you let somebody change you, but I think it depends on how strong-willed you are. I see Beavis and Butthead light one of their friends on fire and I'm not going to do that. Maybe the younger kids who are eight or nine, who don't know any better, may try something like that. But I don't like when people say that music and TV are going to change people."

> "I've seen R-rated movies. I've seen gangs. I've seen drugs. You got to figure out what kind of person you are. You can be changed if you let somebody change you, but I think it depends on how strong-willed you are."—ROMANE

"No offense to Romane," James interjected, "but I think we as Christians deceive ourselves when we say we're not influenced. I think the Bible pretty clearly shows that culture influences us greatly. If you look throughout the Old Testament God placed very strict guidelines on Israel. He was very strict in saying 'Don't let culture shape you. Have nothing to do with evil.'

"If you look at our generation and the entertainment—whether it be music, movies, television or whatever—the generation and entertainment have followed very close paths. If you look at the rash of [teenagers] shooting their classmates, there's no question that these things are results not only of our sin nature but also of these cultural ties. We're vessels of God and we need to remain pure for him in our thoughts, our actions, our deeds, in what we meditate on. That's what

> "In today's society the hero is a big, strong guy with a gun who can take a guy out whenever he wants and who is always going to be on top when the war is over. Teens look at that."—TONY

the Bible calls us to do," he said. "We grossly underestimate the power of sin and the evil in the world. These [incidents] are starting to wake us up to it, but there is no way around it. We are very evil."

"I think kids today want to be accepted," added Tony. "When they're rejected they look for comfort from their parents or friends. But when there aren't parents or friends, they look for a hero. In today's society the hero is a big, strong guy with a gun who can take a guy out whenever he wants and who is always going to be on top when the war is over. They look at that."

"I think along with lacking that guidance," said Mary, "you lose a lot of affirmation. In a kind of self-driven culture where you're only concerned about yourself, there's no room to build other people up. And I think that contributes to a feeling like you have to prove something and not being sure of your own worth. A lot of teens seem not at all convinced that they're worth something."

Vanessa asserted that parents "don't have too much control" over

> "In a kind of self-driven culture where you're only concerned about yourself, there's no room to build other people up. And I think that contributes to a feeling like you have to prove something and not being sure of your own worth. A lot of teens seem not at all convinced that they're worth something."—MARY

their children; they don't "tell them what's right and what's wrong. They don't really know who their friends are—their true friends. That's something that the parents need to control.

"My parents and I get into an argument," she said, "but I don't even think about killing them. I may say something that hurts their feelings, but I apologize for saying that. It's about control," she said. "You

> Parents "don't have too much control" over their children; they don't "tell them what's right and what's wrong."—VANESSA

have to set your foot down and say, 'This is my house.' "

To recap: Donny said that the combination of weak-mindedness and negative role models on TV or in music creates an environment in which young people break down. Romane demurred, suggesting that if a person knows who he or she is, outside forces like TV won't have an impact. James insisted, to the contrary, that the media culture does have an influence and that Christians should keep themselves pure by not exposing themselves to it. Tony felt that the schoolyard shootings were a desperate attempt on the part of these young people to be accepted; they were mimicking the kind of "heroism" that the media upholds. Mary added that many young people today feel as if they don't have worth and therefore need to prove themselves, while at the same time they lack parental guidance. Vanessa said that parents have lost control over their children.

In short, they named the negative influence of media, a need to belong, a feeling of worthlessness and a lack of parental guidance as factors contributing to the crises which culminated in the schoolyard killings.

Boomer Parents

But the parental-control issue can get complicated, as Donny pointed out later in the discussion, "They're basically working just to keep their family living, but they're not home to teach the family how to live. I'm being raised by my mom. She has to raise three kids, three boys. Two of them are starting to rebel, just like I did. And now she's asking me to help her because she wants me to teach them to show more respect."

James said, "In your generation [meaning the baby boomers], the sin nature embodied itself in 'self' and the desire to satisfy yourself. And because you guys are our parents, your generation's emphasis on self has made it so both parents are at work to make the most money possible. So we're being raised without parents in the home, and we don't have that guidance. We're raised by day cares and television and everything else."

"But it's like, what do you do? Do you stay at home and struggle with your life?" protested Romane. "You got to understand, these parents are having a hard time, you know what I'm saying? It's not as easy as you think.

"One time I got in trouble with the gangs and my mom came home and stayed for a week. But she had to go back to work or we would have been put out. She couldn't pay the rent. It's hard for them, especially being a single parent, but even when you got two parents it's hard to make ends meet to live even an okay life. If my mom didn't work, I wouldn't be able to go to school. What kind of situation would I be in then? Everything costs money—going on field trips, lunch. My mom chose to go to work and give us money to do those things other kids were doing.

"When she got home late at night some nights, I used to love it when my mom woke me up and just said, 'How are you doing?' or gave me a big hug. Those are the nights I remember."

Added Vanessa, "As long as the child knows that the parent is there for them when they need them, that's all that really matters. As long as you have God the Lord in your household, you shouldn't worry."

"But the family of the kid who killed his parents [referring to Kip Kinkel] were supposedly very religious, moral people," interjected James. "Yeah, there are traditional mores—kind of like a 'system' of religion—and those things have affected people. But they're not stronger than our sin nature.

"I think most baby boomers today would say they're religious and believe in God," he continued. "They obviously don't act on it—obviously it's just lip service—but they were raised by their parents in the home, and those values were passed on. Since we were not raised by our parents, those values were not passed on," he said. "Now we're breaking down all those walls, and so people are free to exercise their sin nature even more. We're just spiraling down and down. It's sick immorality; it's just disgusting. We believe that we're all good people who were raised poorly or we're good people who watched too much TV. But what I'm saying is we have a sin nature. [These actions are] rooted in our evilness."

Added Tony, "It's like, someone says—so I'm gay. Congress says it's okay. And if you want to legalize marijuana, it's okay—legalize it. Like pornography or the Playboy Channel. It's okay to show it, but you can only show it at night when kids are supposed to be asleep. So that's how they justify what's wrong. Your generation [the baby boomers] had the dream that we should be free to express ourselves and I think a majority of our generation actually live the dream. They do what they want. They feel that what they're doing is okay."

"I was watching *Inside Edition* yesterday," Vanessa chimed in. "This little girl got bullied by some people, so her father sent them lawsuits for fifty thousand dollars. People go on national TV telling their business like you wouldn't want to know—who's sleeping with whom, who's gay, who's not. Kids are looking up to that. If it doesn't come to an end, I hate to see what it is going to be like ten, fifteen, twenty years from now."

Said Mary, "We talk to non-Christian friends about homosexuality or movies, but we really avoid the true issue, which is Christ and his power over that evil. That's what people are hoping to find. Our words can't ultimately have any power over our non-Christian friends. If we lead them to Jesus that is what can make a difference."

The thoughts expressed at this point in the discussion reflected an unstinting recognition on the part of these teens that the role of parents is critical. The fact that the parents of the teens' generation are the baby boomers complicates the picture. Their revolution left many single-parent homes like Donny's in its wake and accelerated consumerism, creating an environment where both parents work to maintain a certain standard of living, as James noted. That is not to say that every family in which one or both parents work has capitulated to materialism. As Romane pointed out, "everything costs money," and some parents who would rather be at home have to work just to pay for hundred-dollar basketball shoes (more fall-out of the consumer culture) or the fifty-dollar backpack that young people have to have.

Vanessa indicated that parental love and the presence of the Lord were all young people needed, though James differentiated between "traditional mores"—religious trappings—and an actual walk with God. Boomers, he said, seemed to give "lip service" to religion without apprehending its total scope. Tony added that what the boomers started is being realized in his generation: everything and anything is "okay." The show *Inside Edition*, said Vanessa, attests to this, betraying how far we have fallen as a culture: when young people and their parents go on national television "telling their business like you wouldn't want to know."

Mary concluded that simply talking about sinful acts that are wrong will not win over this culture. "If we lead them to Jesus," she said, "that is what can make a difference."

And how to do that is what I will explore in the following chapters.

Key Points

☐ Teens today are jumble of contradictions. They struggle with doubt, yet remain righteously indignant; they are jaded, yet hopeful.

☐ They want parents to take charge.

☐ They resent those who pay only "lip service" to religious conviction.

Prayer Point

Thank you, Lord, for the creativity you display in each successive generation. Help young people today find strength in their diversity. Give them a clear vision for your truth and warmed hearts to extend your compassion in their broken worlds. Heal them where their souls have been damaged by the mistakes of their parents.

3

The Power of
the Plug

J uly 19, 1940: Heard Hitler's speech over the radio wherein he
warned England for the last time. He felt sorry for the English
driven by deluded politicians into a war of destruction."

This journal entry, written by my maternal grandmother, Pearl
Bucklen Bentel, captures a glimpse of an age when the media informed
an attentive and news-hungry public about the happenings in the larger
world. In the days of my grandmother the world seemed like a big place
where events unfolded with an air of cosmic significance. Listeners
who sat in their living rooms huddled around the radio seemed like
small players in a large universe. Her journal entry of April 28, 1941,
reads: "Heard Churchill's broadcast on the fall of Greece & evacuation
of R.E. 7 under fire," and of December 7: "War! declared," and of
February 15, 1942: "Churchill's radio talk tells of Singapore's fall."

In his book *PostModerns* Craig Kennet Miller tracks the development of the way information was passed on throughout the twentieth
century.[1] In the early 1900s information came in the form of books,
newspapers and magazines. By the 1920s, 1930s and 1940s commu-
nication had evolved to include radio, records and movies. Television
came into most American homes in the 1950s, heralding a new era in

American culture. As the medium evolved in the 1960s and 1970s, spawning other electronic diversions like cassette tapes and transistor radios, it also became more corrupting. The TV culture today, in conjunction with advances in electronic technology, has become a force that has rewritten the rules about the American way of life.

Miller suggests that the worst aspect of the ascendance of the media culture has been the diminishing parental control over what their kids are exposed to.[2] While this has been one of its effects, I believe there has been another, more damaging, repercussion. When my grandmother listened to Hitler and Churchill on the radio in the 1940s, people waited and watched (and listened) as events unfolded around them and tended to think in terms of how, in their own small way, they could play a role in the larger picture. The world was big and humans were small.

As media have evolved and the world has changed, so has this bigness-smallness ratio. The world was still "big" when television found its way into American homes in the 1950s. But as postwar prosperity collided with the birth of more babies than had heretofore been born in a single generation, an atmosphere was created wherein the TV/entertainment culture not only thrived but exploded. The growing economy introduced leisure, and the media quickly recognized the value of entertaining the masses who suddenly had free time and extra money. This meant capturing viewing allegiances and a burgeoning advertising industry. "Advertising played a big part in shaping [baby boomers'] expectations from an early age," writes Wade Clark Roof in his book *A Generation of Seekers*. "Good economic times, a more consumption-oriented society, and the use of television for mass marketing all came together at just the time when the largest cohort of children ever in America was being born."[3] As a result, the bigness-smallness ratio of how Americans perceived their place in the world began its great reversal.

Susan Littwin, author of *The Postponed Generation*, said that it was difficult to say when "the experimenting" started to turn "sinister."

When the four Kent State University students were killed by Ohio National Guard soldiers in 1970, a journalist at *Time* magazine wrote: "With almost manic abruptness, the nation seemed, as Yeats once wrote, 'all changed, changed utterly.' "[4] It is impossible to pinpoint a moment in time when the baby boomers' revolution turned "sinister." But the Kent State incident captured in one episode the crisis that was besetting the nation: The rule of order found itself unprepared to reckon with the force of the baby boomers' upheaving revolution. In the several years that followed Kent State the voting age was lowered to eighteen, abortion was legalized, and the Watergate scandal gained momentum. Confidence in overarching authorities was shattering while the free-spirited, rights-oriented baby boomers emerged *en masse* onto the social scene. Their sheer numbers made them a force to be reckoned with. And their revolution elevated individual freedoms, self-expression, the loss of inhibition and the ridicule of authority. The prerogative of individual human will asserted itself while the sense about one's humble place in the larger world dwindled. In other words, humans became big while the world at large became small.

The electronic media collided with these social forces and seemed to become both an extension of and a force that continued to shape this great reversal. "More than any other medium," writes Roof, "television shaped consumer tastes and raised their level of expectations for the future. . . . By the time the average boomer had reached sixteen years of age, television had captured an estimated 12,000 to 15,000 hours of his or her time."[5] Television became, the author concludes, "the major source of information shaping their definitions of reality, exceeding that of books, newspapers, teachers, religious leaders, perhaps supplanting the family itself."[6]

Television assumed a place of influence and to some degree became the standard-bearer for culture as the baby boomers came of age. And since television was fast becoming a medium driven by consumerism, the boomers found themselves at the center of their own cultural universe. No longer were individuals small players in a bigger picture—they *were the picture*. Rather than reflect upon what they could contribute to their world, boomers forced the question: What did their world offer *them?*

This wouldn't have been a bad thing if the boomers' revolution had created the utopian picture they envisioned: love, love, love and all that. But—as we are only now realizing—the boomers' cultural ethos created a world for their offspring that was in many respects, in the words of Diana West in the *Wall Street Journal,* "a social experiment gone awry."[7]

> Boomers found themselves at the center of their own cultural universe. No longer were individuals small players in a bigger picture—they *were the picture.* Rather than reflect upon what they could contribute to their world, boomers forced the question: What did their world offer *them?*

The social environment today reflects skepticism about absolutes and the loss of a sense of a bigger picture. This incredulity and isolation have been fleshed out in those who are absorbing the brunt of the baby boomers' revolution: their offspring.

Generation X

Shana was born in 1971 to a young working mom whose marriage fell apart and whose husband left the family. Shana's mom was left to raise her three children alone. Because her mom was consumed with working in order to pay the bills, Shana had to make her own way through her teenage years. She worked throughout high school to save for her college education, she chose the college she would attend, and she applied for and paid her own student loans. While in college she met Zack, a computer whiz who had mastered the medium, having been raised on video games.

Shana and Zack fell in love and decided to get married. Zack, who did not yet have a full-time job, bought Shana an expensive engagement ring, and they went on a cruise for their honeymoon.

Since their marriage, Shana has worked full time and Zack has started his own computer consulting business working from their home. They have no kids but plan to when Shana is ready. The way Zack describes it, Shana has worked hard to get where she is and she wants to enjoy the fruit of her labor before children come into their life, because then, she anticipates, her working life will have to be adapted in order to meet the needs of the children. Shana and Zack have been slowly building a savings account, thanks to Shana's financial discipline which she acquired during her youth, though they maintain a hefty monthly credit card debt.

Despite having been raised without any church background, Shana and Zack wanted to belong to a church and made persistent attempts to find a congregation where they felt at home. They settled on a small church in the Methodist tradition. Shana has been involved in preparing meals for the homeless at a nearby shelter, and Zack was recently asked to become an elder because many who served on the board were advanced in years and they wanted new blood.

Shana, more than Zack, is always vigilant to remember birthdays of nieces and nephews in Zack's extended family. One year for Christmas she sent each of Zack's siblings a Christmas ornament with a note that read: "Please place this ornament on your tree and, each year, think of how blessed we are to have this wonderful family."

At one important juncture, however, when Zack's extended family faced the crisis of a sibling's divorce, Shana initially responded with compassion but eventually suggested that Zack just get over it. Divorce isn't the end of the world, she said.

This couple is a fair representation of what it means to belong to Generation X, the first wave of boomer offspring (born between 1965 and 1976). This group bore the initial shock of the paradigm shift—the inverted bigness-smallness ratio—that occurred as their parents came of age. "An awakening era that seemed euphoric to young adults was, to them, a nightmare of self-immersed parents, disintegrating homes, schools with conflicting missions, confused leaders, a culture shifting from G to R ratings, new public health dangers, and a Me Decade economy that tipped toward the organized old and away from the voiceless young. 'Grow up fast' was the adult message," note Strauss and Howe in *Generations*.[8] In this sense Gen Xers are America's true children of the 1960s.

No other generation has seen such a dramatic surge in mothers with young children entering the work force. Between 1960 and 1980 the percentage of mothers with children under the age of five who held either full- or part-time jobs rose from twenty to forty-seven percent; the number of latchkey kids under the age of fourteen doubled through the 1970s.

> Generation X, the first wave of boomer offspring, bore the initial shock of the paradigm shift that occurred as their parents came of age.

Generation X is the age group that has been hit the hardest with divorce. Gen Xers in the mid-1980s faced twice the likelihood of parents divorcing as did the boomers in the 1960s. They have been the most aborted generation in U.S. history, and they are the most heavily incarcerated generation in American history.[9]

Unlike the boomers, who emerged into adulthood in the context of affluence, Generation X "lurched through the recession of the early '80s only to see the mid-decade glitz dissipate in the 1987 stock-market crash and the recession of 1990-91."[10] They are the first generation to have come of age using computers with the same frequency that the previous generation used the telephone.[11] They also came of age when corporate downsizing sacrificed forty-three million jobs.[12] Federal grants for college tuition were cut back, which meant that one out of three Gen Xers held jobs to earn money while they were attending school. And on top of this, despite the skyrocketing cost of a college education, parents of Gen Xers helped less with college costs than did their own parents. A 1991 national survey revealed that only one quarter of Gen Xers (26 percent) said their parents paid for more than one fifth of their college expenses.[13] This might also might explain why many Gen Xers are taking five years to complete their college education.[14]

This has made them, among other things, a generation of borrowers. But this has as much to do with growing up in a consumer culture as it does with college loans. Gen Xers "have no qualms about using credit to pay for comfort or even luxury," writes Joshua Wolf Shenk in *U.S. News & World Report*.[15] The moral imperative to live within one's means, he says, seems "as distant as the Great Depression." The average outstanding credit bill for households headed by people under twenty-five grew from $885 to $1,721 between 1990 and 1995.[16]

A heavier debt burden coupled with a propensity to spend has meant that many Gen Xers are looking for the fast track to high-paying jobs. Rather than majoring in literature or philosophy, many college students are pursuing more specialized majors. Desiree Saylor, a senior at the University of Texas, wanted to pursue a career as a physical anthropologist, but her sixteen thousand dollar debt compelled her to get a degree in occupational therapy instead.[17]

At the same time, Gen Xers long for community and relationships. A sense of belonging at church, for example, is more important than hearing a good sermon or listening to outstanding music. Shana and Zack wanted to attend the small Methodist church rather than any of the larger, more polished congregations they visited.

Whatever the baby boomers intended, the end result of their revolution has meant a lot of heartache for Generation X. "Xers look at what [the boomers] actually did," says J. Walker Smith, managing partner of Yankelovich Partners, "Divorce. Latchkey kids. Homelessness. Soaring national debt. Holes in the ozone layer. Crack. Downsizing and layoffs. Urban deterioration. Gangs. Junk bonds."[18]

Shana grew up understanding that if she was going to get anything out of life, no one was going to hand it to her. This empowered and emboldened her to set her own course, work hard, enjoy the benefits of her success and refuse to be set back by life's hard knocks. Her longing for community and relationships is exhibited in their church choice and her vigilance to remember birthdays. The hard edge that typifies so many who belong to Generation X is evident in her suggestion that Zack "get over" his sister's divorce; her joy at "belonging" to a large and loving family is captured in the message she enclosed with the Christmas ornament.

Millennials

Buffy the Vampire Slayer is smart and in control, says thirteen-year-old Anna-Lucille Calabrese.[19] Buffy is the heroine of the popular teen television show of the same name, and she has a mission: "When the bloodsuckers emerge, she must be there to make mincemeat out of them."[20] Buffy is a teen hero who resembles many of her television peers. The context in which she lives her life includes "an absurdly clueless parent" and the "insularity of suburbia."

Teen television programs reflect a subtle shift in the mindset of the second wave of baby-boomer offspring, the Millennials. In many of these programs the teens, for all their exaggerated hormonal surges, emerge as the ones who make sense, exert traditionalistic impulses and win the day. Another popular teen program, *Dawson's Creek,* portrays the lead character, Dawson Leery, as an upright young man with common sense who faces a conflicted world. At one point one of his female friends tries to baptize strait-laced Dawson into the *real* teen world by encouraging him to shoplift. Dawson refuses. At another point his baby-boomer parents have allowed their marriage to devolve from the mother's affair to the parents' attempt at reconciliation, to the father's idea to try an "open marriage," to their overall failure to recoup lost ground. Dawson's father moves out and files for divorce. In the tangle of emotions and conversations, Dawson says to his wayward and confused father, "I don't want a friend. I want a father."

The no-nonsense Buffy and the searching, upright Dawson help to draw a contrast between Generation X and the Millennials. The second wave of baby-boom offspring share many of the same cultural demographics as their Gen X forebears (divorce rates of their parents are still high, for example), but there is one critical difference. Generation X grew up *enmeshed* in their parents' revolution, while the Millennials are growing up *reacting to* the revolution.

When Generation X came of age, baby boomers embraced and justified their revolution. Divorce, day care and free expression were considered good things—or at least not bad things. But as the Millennials emerge into adolescence, the results are coming in: aspects of the revolution have gone awry. Barbara Dafoe Whitehead writes a cover story for *Atlantic Monthly* that asserts "Dan Quayle Was Right,"[21] and *Time* magazine runs a cover story called "The Myth of Quality Time."[22] Says William Strauss, "The Millennial generation is coming of cognitive age at a time when the adult community has determined the conditions of childhood to be unacceptable."[23]

For the purposes of this book I am focusing on those "conditions of childhood" that center on the influence of the electronic media culture. This is the world that has shaped the Millennial generation. It has been described by one social critic as "inescapable, omnivorous, and self-referring."[24] Television, computer technology and music together are leaving an imprint on the inner disposition of today's young people.

Television. A notable example of trends in television can be found in the wild success of Comedy Central's cartoon *South Park*. In the last two weeks of February 1998, 5.2 million people tuned in to it (a huge audience by cable standards), with 23 percent of the audience under the age of eighteen. Characters include Wendy Testaberger, who causes another character to throw up every time she talks to him; Kenny, who dies a violent death in each episode; Mrs. Cartman, a promiscuous mom whom the kids call "a 'crack whore' and 'dirty slut' "; and Mr. Hankey, an imaginary singing and dancing "Christmas poo" (that's poo, not Pooh). *South Park* has "broken our sweetest taboo and revealed childhood as a dangerous and obscene place."[25]

Some say the show "hits a generational funny bone," while others call it the result of "a soulless country raising soulless kids."[26] But souls and funny bones aside, AT&T, Calvin Klein and Snapple each paid eighty thousand dollars for a thirty-second commercial slot (twenty times Comedy Central's original rate-card costs), and T-shirt sales have topped thirty million dollars. More than 250 unofficial web sites have opened up, the largest of which received over two million hits within its first year.[27] *South Park* satisfies the consuming market.

Other shows like *Snuff TV* and *Shockumentaries* reflect the "intensely competitive environment" for capturing viewers. "As their share of the audience erodes, the networks are harder pressed to come up with the sort of programming that arrests viewers midsurf. Ten years ago, you wouldn't have been able to do these shows," writes Mike Darnell in *Rolling Stone*.[28]

The shock levels, what David Denby calls the "sheer cruddiness" of some aspects of the medium, have, in his words, perpetuated "the acceptance of a degraded environment that devalues everything."[29] One teen told me that on television so many things are seen as "normal" that it's hard to know what is "really right." Another teen wrote in his school newspaper that television is

> "As their share of the audience erodes, the networks are harder pressed to come up with the sort of programming that arrests viewers midsurf. Ten years ago, you wouldn't have been able to do these shows."—*Rolling Stone's* MIKE DARNELL

"a drug so powerful it cultivates millions of users around the world each year [and] practically everyone is addicted. I know I am."[30]

Computers. The second arm of the electronic media that is having an impact on our young is computer technology.

There are so many benefits and blessings that attend the ever-evolving computer industry that it is easy to overlook the kind of impact this world has on the inner dispositions of young people. Teens today are growing up with a command of computer technology that in many cases surpasses that of their parents. Even when young people do not have access to a computer at home, public schools have made computer labs as prevalent as biology labs. According to a *Newsweek* poll, 89 percent of teens said they use a computer at least several times a week, 61 percent surf the Internet, 92 percent think computers will improve their educational opportunities, 71 percent would prefer to talk into their computers rather than type, and 98 percent credit computer technology for making a positive impact on their lives.[31]

Statistics from the U.S. Department of Labor in 1996 revealed that fifty thousand teens between the ages of sixteen and nineteen held part-time computer-related jobs (compared to four thousand a decade ago).[32] Compaq computers offered Trent Eisenberg a job at their corporate headquarters after he impressed them with his technical advice, but were forced to withdraw the offer when they discovered that Eisenberg was only fourteen.[33]

But there is a downside to all these blessings. The other day when I retrieved e-mail, my screen lit up in psychedelic greens and blues advertising (in large print): "Live Cybersex, Right On Your Computer Screen! (Click Here to Order.)"

"Under the tolerant auspices of the World Wide Web, any child of nine sitting at a computer in Medford, Oregon, or Opa-Locka, Florida, can explore the landscape of sexual deviance first mapped by the Marquis de Sade."[34] The Internet remains an unfiltered frontier for youth who navigate cyberspace.

There is also an addictive aspect to this medium. David Denby's teenage son Max, on Saturdays or over vacation, will "hit the computer" as soon as he gets up, "ignoring bowls of cereal placed under his nose as he plays one of the war-strategy games that he currently loves." The computer games, he says, offer a "kind of narrative . . . that yields without resistance to the child's desire for instant gratification."[35]

Have you ever noticed how the spell-checkers in many word-processing programs today are devoid of religious terminology? That is because words like *missiology* and *ecclesiology,* even in some cases *evangelical,* do not exist in the worldviews of the people who write these programs. Bill Gates himself once said that he does not attend church because he does not have time for "religion." (There is a lot you can get done on a Sunday morning, he says.) Spell-checkers and

Gates's lack of worship habits reflect a void that exists in this realm. It is created and sustained by people who do not factor God into their thinking.

Many Christians are making inroads and are keeping up with the industry in their programming, but the industry itself seems to lack a transcendent sense of who God is. In fact, it could be argued that some view the technological realm itself as a new belief system. "The printing press starts with Bibles and ends up with pulp fiction. Radio popularizes rock 'n' roll. TV spawns the sitcom. Now consider the possibilities that will open up as the computer meets the Net . . . the Net of a hundred years from now, when media can move at the speed of light," writes Joshua Quittner. "Deus ex machina. Amen."[36]

Music. A third arm of the electronic media is the music culture. Some suggest that alternative music is on the wane; if it is, it has deferred to its grittier, raunchier offspring—industrial music. Both the more reflective (albeit morose) alternative and the harsher industrial music capture aspects of the spirit of the age: dark, edgy, unresolved and off key. A drummer for an alternative band, interviewed by Craig Miller for his book *PostModerns,* said, "I have to keep the rhythm going but the other instruments will play off it by not being quite in beat. . . . Alternative singers don't have great voices."[37] Nihilism and, in some cases, sadism pervade this music culture, reflected in the self-mutilation of many of its adherents. "Cutting," tattooing, body piercing and other forms of self-inflicted abuse reflect the degradation this subculture perpetuates.

This has carried over into a troubling secondary aspect of the music culture: "heroin chic." The number of alternative-band heroes who have overdosed, been arrested for possession, admitted use of heroin or recovered from heroin abuse is "staggering," notes Karen Schoemer in *Newsweek.*[38] They include members of the bands Nirvana, Hole, Smashing Pumpkins, Everclear, Blind Melon, Skinny Puppy, 7 Year Bitch, Red Hot Chili Peppers, Stone Temple Pilots, the Breeders, Alice in Chains, Sublime, Sex Pistols, Porno for Pyros and Depeche Mode.

"Together these bands have sold more than 60 million albums—that's a heck of a lot of white, middle-class kids in the heartland."[39]

Heroin consumption in the United States has doubled since the mid-1980s. In 1995 it had reached ten to fifteen metric tons a year, and in 1995 2.3 percent of *eighth-graders* said they had tried it (nearly double the rate in 1991).[40] "Baby boomer parents may be shocked by the new casual attitude toward heroin, which even in the drug days of the '60s carried a stigma that seemed to set it apart from pot, acid, and the Summer of Love."[41] Today it is considered the drug of convenience. Whereas the heroin boomer parents consumed had to be cooked before it was injected, today's heroin comes in a more sophisticated powdered form, so that users only have to "bust some lines of it."

This is only a snapshot of our young people's world, and it certainly does not paint the whole picture. There remain a lot of happy places in their world. As will be discussed later, many young people display a remarkable resilience and ability to transcend and transform aspects of the culture. Nevertheless, it is incumbent upon parents, pastors and educators to reckon with the dark side of the media culture which is very much part of the world they inhabit and to recognize that pop culture has left its mark on this generation. Young people today, according to David Denby, "are shaped by the media as consumers before they've had a chance to develop their souls."[42]

When the Lights Went Out

The one time in my life when I had to confront how shamelessly dependent on electricity I had become occurred during the last year my family and I lived in Honduras, in 1994. The country's main water supply came from a reservoir called El Cajon. Honduras is no larger than the state of Tennessee, so it is not inconceivable that the electricity for the entire country was generated by one dam. The water levels in the reservoir were becoming dangerously low. Since it was only the beginning of the dry season, there was little hope for relief anytime soon.

When the lights started to go out in sporadic intervals in January

1994, we quickly learned how dependent these poor countries were on rainfall. These frustrating, exasperating and unpredictable blackouts quickly evolved into regularly scheduled rolling blackouts, at first every other day, but soon every day. The electric company tried not to extend the blackouts in any given neighborhood for more than four or five hours. But soon the plan had to be adapted, and we were facing up to eight hours every day without electricity.

For us, no electricity meant more than no TV or computer time. We also had no water. The water in our home came from a cistern outside, and the water from the cistern was channeled into our pipes by means of an electric pump. So during the tediously long stretches when we were called on to do our part in preserving the country's water supply in El Cajon, we could not watch television, work on the computer, wash dishes, flush toilets, do laundry, sit under a spinning fan in the heat of the day, wash the sweat from our faces or even open the refrigerator to get a drink of water.

During daylight hours our life was reduced to reading books and playing board games, and during nighttime hours to reading books and playing board games by candlelight. We went to bed at obscenely early hours, sometimes only to be aroused in the middle of the night by glaring lights when the electricity would come back on unexpectedly.

> You quickly take stock of your life when everything around you is unplugged.

You quickly take stock of your life when everything around you is unplugged.

Since we've returned to live in the United States, I've marveled at how lost we'd all be if our country were to confront the kind of electricity crisis that Honduras experienced. Nearly everything we do in the course of a day is predicated on an uninterrupted electricity supply. The fear that drives the Y2K frenzy is a good measure of how far we've come in our dependency.

I have never forgotten the lessons I learned during those hard days in Honduras. We aren't playing board games as much, but we are comfortable sitting in a quiet room without stimulation from a glowing, droning box. There is a quiescence that attends this freedom that we might not have apprehended had we not been forced to wean ourselves of our electronic dependency.

When David Denby thinks about what he calls this electronic kiddies' bouillabaisse and how it is impacting his teenage son Max, he laments, "There is so much to forbid. Perhaps the whole culture to forbid! How do you control what they breathe? What [are] the internal injuries along the way?

"It is a miserable question."[43]

Key Points

□ The evolving media culture has led to a loss of parental control over what kids see, hear and learn about.

□ The media perpetuate the notion that individual human wants and freedoms are the epicenter of the cultural universe.

□ Generation X has borne the brunt of the baby boomers' cultural revolution of the 1960s.

□ Generation X came of age enmeshed in their parents' revolution, while Millennials are growing up reacting to it.

□ The shock element on television has reached levels that would have been unheard of ten years ago.

□ The leader of the computer industry, Bill Gates, does not have time for "religion."

□ Degradation and heroin chic are heralded and glorified as heroic in much of today's music.

□ Picture your world without electricity. What is left?

Prayer Point

Lord, help us to find wholeness in aspects of life that do not require an electrical outlet. Deliver our young people from the lies perpetuated by those who degrade and dishonor your name.

4

What We Didn't Anticipate

When the electronic media, so much of which is driven by consumerism, defines a culture, the world can become a disorienting place. The evidence of this is measurable in the two generations that followed the baby boomers and have borne the brunt of the effects of their revolution: Generation X and the Millennials. Generation X emerged in a time when the verdict hadn't come in as to the effects of the inverted bigness-smallness ratio, but the Millennials are coming of age when the effects are more evident: aspects of the revolution have failed, or at least have not reached its utopian aspirations. It's time to reassess—and reassessment has brought to light some additional unintended effects.

For the purposes of this book I have identified four unintended effects that have left an imprint on today's young people. The first is the result of their near-constant exposure to an electronic "haze": lulling of the creative process and fragmentation of thought patterns and the ways they process information. The second is moral ambivalence that is the fallout of consumer-oriented perceptions of the world. This has contributed to the third effect: spiritual languishing. The distortion of what is considered normal has created a longing for meaning beyond human appetites and impulses. All of these have combined to create the fourth unintended effect: a collective shift in society's psychological center of gravity. Media saturation, moral ambivalence and attendant spiritual longing have triggered societal resolve to make things better. This is the context in which our youth are coming of age and the reason that the time is ripe for the believing community to seize the moment and capture their allegiance.

The Electronic Haze

In December 1997 the *Washington Times* ran a story about a TV cartoon in Japan that had to be pulled off the air because some seven hundred children had to be hospitalized after watching the "mesmerizing animation."[1] According to the story, the "action-packed" cartoon called Pokemon was canceled when the brilliantly flashing scenes were blamed for causing "convulsions, spasms or nausea in hundreds of children."[2] Japanese cartoons over the past several years had developed "unforgiving packages of fast-paced action that require intense concentration to be understood," the article said, resulting in some children hyperventilating and others developing signs of brain seizures. Said one mother, "I was shocked to see my daughter lose consciousness."[3]

This is an extreme but fitting metaphor for the crippling effects of excessive exposure to an electronically stimulating environment. Some of these effects include the following:

Passivity and addiction to speed and shock. "The language of video art has infiltrated the real world—via amusement arcades, Internet ads, MTV—and we are all native speakers," writes Andrew Solomon in the *New York Times Magazine.*[4] As the media culture has bombarded American youth with a barrage of visual, digital and other forms of electronic stimulation, psychologists are seeing more and more cases of stress caused by "information overload" and the "noxious environment of overstimulation."[5]

The glut of information has forced advertisers to reach their audiences with a streamlined hard-hitting pitch. MTV sustains images on the screen for no longer than ten seconds, and radio and TV stations are selling commercial time for as little as ten or twenty seconds.[6] "If there is an ultimate limit to the pace of entertainment we must now be approaching it," writes James Gleick in his article "Addicted to Speed."[7] NBC 2000 is developing a way to diminish the "blacks" (the barely traceable instant when a show fades to black before introducing a commercial) in order to keep the restless, remote-happy viewer engaged. "Give the viewer a full second of blank screen," he writes, "and your thumb starts to squeeze the change-channel button."[8]

Channel surfing has created a demand for quicker and more shocking images to capture the viewer. "This, in turn, is leading to less satisfaction with programs as a whole, which of course promotes more rapid channel surfing."[9] The results are shortened attention spans, elevated impatience and a craving for continual stimulation. James Gorman, deputy science editor of the *New York Times,* writes: "There's an argument to be made that the defining characteristic of human life is not language or tool use but the development of remote control."[10]

> Channel surfing has created a demand for quicker and more affecting images to capture the viewer.

Isolation. An additional result of this electronic environment is a tendency to miss opportunities for neighborly, leisurely paced human engagement. This contributes to a sense of isolation and disconnection from community. In an information society "we spend ever greater portions of our lives sitting in chairs, staring at screens," writes Mark Dery in the *New York Times Magazine.* "Voice mail and E-mail are gradually supplanting face-to-face interaction and embodied experience is giving way to electronic immersion in virtual worlds."[11] A high-school senior told me that she finds comfort sitting in front of her computer screen because she can "bury her pain in its comforting anonymity."

A distorted view of reality. TV sitcoms and the advertising industry

> A high-school senior told me that she finds comfort sitting in front of her computer screen because she can "bury her pain in its comforting anonymity."

perpetuate fantasies. Life is meant to be fun; you deserve to be happy. This fosters an attitude of ingratitude when life is not fun, as well as a futile quest to take hold of happiness, which is usually defined by the media culture in consumerist terms. All of this undercuts a larger worldview.[12] Life's difficulties are confronted and resolved in the span of a half-hour, and rarely are consequences to amoral choices meted out in the lives of the characters (the final episode of *Seinfeld* notwithstanding). This perpetuates an artificial, short-term outlook on the manageability of life's struggles. Suffering is something that must be resolved or avoided. It is seldom seen as redeeming. Life on TV neglects to factor in a larger world view and the sense that there might be something more important than immediate gratification and resolution. Louise, age thirteen, says that "part of being alive is being able to enjoy [life], and if you can't enjoy it anymore, then what's the point?"[13]

The lulling effects of the media have been noted by college professors who have confronted unprecedented levels of apathy and a loss of initiative in the classroom. A survey conducted annually[14] by the Higher Education Research Institute at the University of California at Los Angeles reveals that college freshman during the 1997-1998 academic year reported "record levels of academic and civic apathy."[15]

More colleges boast easy access to computer technology for their student bodies, but there remains a marked shortage of career-track computer programmers. "Our children tend to be overweight, visually over-stimulated, and academically under-stimulated," says journalist Tom Ehrich. "College students set up their dorm rooms like entertainment centers."[16]

University of Virginia professor Mark Edmundson bemoans "the attitude of calm consumer expertise" that pervades student evaluations of his class on Freud, "as if my function—and, more important, Freud's or Shakespeare's or Blake's—is to divert, entertain, and interest." When a student praised him for making this difficult material "enjoyable," Edmundson responded, "Thanks but no thanks." He explains: "I don't teach to amuse."[17]

My friend J. I. Packer visits our home when he comes to town on his many business trips. During one of his more recent visits, he agreed to participate in our son Ben's small Bible-study group. These young men came loaded with questions that addressed how young people can live a Christian life in the context of today's culture. One of the questions they raised was, "How involved do you think we should be in secular entertainment like music and television?" Packer's answer offers sage advice:

All work and no play makes Jack a dull boy. That's an old British proverb and it's true, of course. If there's no place in your life for relaxation and entertainment and fun, you are going to be a very dull chap.

So what do you do? The principle that applies here is the principle of six days work followed by one day rest. In the week as God reveals it, you have six days work and one day's rest. That gives a proportion of one-to-six, which means entertainment would be something like 15 percent of your time. Think it through in terms of an ordinary day. You're going to do an ordinary day at school, and you've got homework to do. There's nothing inappropriate about one hour of entertainment.

Don't become a couch potato and sit watching television for six or seven hours together. That's letting entertainment get out of hand, and it takes the bloom off all your life. By simply sitting around soaking up what you're being fed, you don't get the pleasure of doing things for yourself—hard work, creative hobbies, good sport.[18]

Someone else asked, "What about R-rated movies?" He answered:

The practical principle which is very important for a Christian is: You share everything with the Lord. You see his blessing in everything you do. You try to keep out of your life things that you can't offer to him and thank him for. And you discuss with him the life experiences that he's given you and ask him regularly, "Lord, what am I going to learn from this?"

That's real, practical, down-to-earth, nitty-gritty Christianity.[19]

American culture writ large does not usually engage the mind of J. I. Packer on these issues. The loss of initiative, creativity and enthusiasm on college campuses and in high-school classrooms is symptomatic of a society that has glutted itself with consumerism and entertainment. This has set the stage for the next unintended effect.

Moral Ambivalence

An urban youth named Joe Zefran, eighteen, asked some suburban teens, "What is it like [in the suburbs]? What do you do?"

"Oh, I go to the mall, smoke pot and have sex . . . see a movie once in a while."

Zefran concluded, "So it's boring out in the suburbs because that's what I hear."[20]

Time magazine recently ran an article describing two sexually active fourteen year olds who wandered into a teen center in suburban Salt Lake City wanting to know how to achieve a more fulfilling orgasm. They asked, "How do we get to the G-spot?"[21]

In October 1997 the country was stunned to learn that sixteen-year-old Luke Woodham had stabbed his mother to death and then gone to his school and opened fire, killing two more people. Eight months later, in June 1998, a freckle-faced fifteen year old named Philip Kinkel stabbed his parents and then, wearing a trench coat and armed with a .22 caliber rifle, fired over fifty rounds into a crowd of four hundred of his schoolmates gathered in the cafeteria. This too stunned the nation. But more troubling than the episode itself was the fact that this murder spree involving a minor—a *child*—represented the sixth time in eight months that a student opened fire on fellow classmates in a public school setting. A *U.S. News* article notes, "It wasn't even the only schoolyard killing *last week.*"[22] Add to these the recent massacre at Columbia High School in Littleton, Colorado, and we as a nation remain sobered and confounded by what has gone wrong in the psycho-spiritual dispositions of today's youth.

All of these examples betray a moral disconnection that is occurring in a lot of young people today. Part of the problem is what some social critics are calling "the loss of childhood" in American culture. "At a time when a Texas legislator can propose the death penalty be extended to 11 year olds (and be taken seriously), when children commit ghastly murders and adults struggle to get in touch with their inner child, when first graders run on schedules as rigid and focused as corporate CEOs, and CEOs go to camp to bond

> Part of the problem is what some social critics are calling "the loss of childhood" in American culture.

and climb mountains together, the blurring of the lines of commerce reflect the blurring of the stages of life," writes Peter Applebome in the *New York Times.*[23]

Applebome cites the research of Kiku Adatto, director of the Children's Studies Program at Harvard University, which compares photographic images of children through the decades. From the time of the earliest daguerreotypes through the 1960s, pictures of children evoke innocence and purity. "That has given way to increasingly sexualized images of ever-younger childlike models in ads for products like Obsession cologne or Calvin Klein underwear."[24]

This evolution is due in no small part to the influence of the media. Applebome adds,

> As they grow up physically faster, children are exposed to the world at an ever-accelerated pace. Once parents could pretty well control what children were exposed to. Indeed, the modern notion of childhood depended largely on the withholding of information about sex, about violence, about the adult world that guarded youthful innocence. Now, with television everywhere and second-graders Internet-literate, that is almost impossible.[25]

More young people at younger ages are regularly exposed to adult themes and situations through their television sets or on the Internet. Prepubescent kids are gravitating to movies intended for teens, and teens are going to movies designed for adults. One entertainment researcher has noted that in one upscale Los Angeles neighborhood, "there's no shortage of eight-, nine-, 10- and 11-year-olds" going to R-rated movies. "More than ever, kids seem to be heading to movies intended for the next age group up."[26]

This has placed our children in the unlikely position of being shamelessly exposed to the nitty-gritty realities of a morally vacuous adult world, while still possessing their childlike outlook and emotional faculties. Writes Applebome, "A recent New York Times/CBS News poll of American teenagers found them worldly in ways previous generations were not, but sharing most of the values and sensibilities of earlier times."[27] These conflicting realities account for some of the moral confusion our young people face today.

But the inverted bigness-smallness ratio mentioned in chapter three has also contributed to this moral confusion. Beyond adult themes and images, the media culture also perpetuates the notion that we, the consumers, have the right to good feelings. This breeds ingratitude because life does not always translate into good feelings, and this ingratitude can devolve into resentment and hostility. Add to this the constant exposure to ever-intensifying shock (and the attendant desensitization) and the lack of parental guidance (sadly the case in many homes), and the result is a harvest of young people who bring consumer nonchalance to moral issues like sex, drugs and even killing. It is drummed into them that they are the center of the consuming universe, and so without moral constraints or parental oversight, many cannot assimilate failure or calamity when that universe does not fit the formula.

When assistant principal Joel Myrick subdued Luke Woodham, he kept asking, "Why? Why? Why?"

The boy answered, "Mr. Myrick, the world has wronged me."[28]

If the world "wrongs" them and if they do not have a moral framework within which to process their pain, in moments of mental or emotional crisis those who have serious instabilities most easily defer to the response mechanisms that have been drummed into them through the games they play or the shows they watch. Professor Edmundson notes, "The TV medium is inhospitable to inspiration, improvisation, failures, slipups. What happens if our most intelligent students never learn to strive to overcome what they are?"[29]

"Without the strength and frame of a moral order—some code or rule or custom that provides them with a way and a place to stand against the flood of their own incoherent desire—they too often lose the chance to love or have meaning in their lives," writes Lewis Lapham in an essay in *Harper's*. "If the lights must never go out and the music must always play, how do we even begin to talk about the discovery or construction of such a thing as a new moral order?

"Who has time for so slow a conversation? Who could hear what was being said?"[30]

Spiritual Longing

Moral ambiguity has aroused a yearning to belong to something bigger and greater than the appetites we serve but can't satiate. This has awakened spiritual longings.

Pastor and author Eugene Peterson says that spirituality is "the attention we give to our souls, to the invisible interior of our lives that is the core of our identity, these image-of-God souls that comprise our uniqueness and glory."[31]

For many, spirituality has been lost—or at least pushed out of the picture to be replaced by the artificial stimulation of the media world we surround ourselves with. This is what Denby means when he says that pop culture is turning our young people into consumers before they've had a chance to develop their souls. It is what J. I. Packer means when he says that watching too much television takes the bloom out of your life. "The world for all its vaunted celebration of sensuality is relentlessly anesthetic," writes Peterson, "obliterating feelings by ugliness and noise, draining the beauty out of people."[32]

Shortly before thirty-nine members of the Heaven's Gate cult sought salvation on the tail of Hale-Bopp in the spring of 1997, they posted an e-mail message that asked, "Ready to die for God?"[33]

> **Spiritual questions—whether about the existence of God or about life after death—command the attention of a majority of teens.**

Apparently, yes. One woman who committed suicide with the group said in her farewell video, "They had a formula of how to get out of the human kingdom to a level above humans. And I said to myself, 'That's what I want. That's what I've been looking for.' "[34]

Michael Novak, in an editorial in the *New York Times,* comments that Norman Mailer and Václav Havel—both "ripe with years and not particularly known as pious men"—recently expressed a longing for spiritual answers. Mailer said, "Religion to me is the final frontier," while Havel noted that the "crisis of moral responsibility" we are facing today is due to the fact that we are living in "the first atheistic civilization in the history of humankind." The crisis of faith, says Novak, is the result of the absence of a sense that "the Universe, nature, existence and our lives are the work of a creation guided by a definite intention."[35]

Researchers found a "remarkable convergence of opinion" among religious leaders, seminary presidents, writers and social commentators who concur that America is undergoing a time of "individual and social reassessment, renewal and redirection" while experiencing a "deepening spiritual hunger."[36] This longing is especially acute in much of the teen population, as noted in a recent survey taken by the Princeton Religion Research Center.[37] Spiritual questions—whether about the existence of God or about life after death—command the attention of a majority of teens.

"Our senses require healing and rehabilitation so that they are adequate for receiving and responding to visitations and appearances of Spirit, God's Holy Spirit," writes Peterson.[38] This longing for healing and rehabilitation has helped shape the outlook of the Millennial generation and has set the stage for the fourth unintended effect of the media culture: a change in the psychological center of gravity, to be covered in the next chapter.

Key Points

☐ The pervasiveness of the electronic media environment has had some unanticipated side effects in the lives of today's young people.

☐ The way young people receive and process information has been influenced by shock and speed. Young people are being trained to satisfy their cravings for more shock and speed by pushing a remote control button.

☐ Some might feel more at home in front of a computer screen than in the front yard playing a game of kick-the-can with neighborhood kids.

☐ American culture is reaching the point at which some cultural critics are concluding that a proper sense of "childhood" has been lost.

☐ Young people are continually exposed to adult issues while processing them in a child's emotional framework. This leaves them morally confused.

☐ The artificial environment of the electronic media anesthetizes the soul and shuts out the voice of God.

Prayer Point

Lord, help us slow down the pace and turn down the volume of our world. Give us ears to hear your voice and hearts that are willing to listen and act. Give us the moral courage to engage only in those activities for which we can give you thanks. Help us to be grateful and may our gratitude inspire our youth.

5

What Hath Bob Dole to Do with South Park?

The cultural environment in which our youth are coming of age, where levels of visual, auditory and technological stimulation are ratcheted up, has triggered a surprising, if not contradictory, positive effect. There exists an undercurrent of indignation on the part of many of today's teens. According to William Strauss and Neil Howe, today's Millennial teens—the ones who perfected tongue piercing, who dance in the mosh pit and who made the South Park creators millionaires—are to become the next "civic" generation cut from the cloth of Bob Dole.[1]

> Today's Millennial teens—the ones who perfected tongue piercing, who dance in the mosh pit and who made the South Park creators millionaires—are to become, according to William Strauss and Neil Howe, the next "civic" generation cut from the cloth of Bob Dole.

How Can This Be?

The baby boomers are confronting the fruits of their revolution in the faces of their offspring and are becoming alarmed. And since whatever issues boomers care about influences cultural attention to those issues (for better or worse), their concern has triggered a national effort to once again strengthen parental protection, says William Strauss.[2] As one Gen Xer puts it, "According to the boomer law of cultural tyranny, if the boomers are having families, then we must all turn our attention to the problems of families."[3] Parents and society at large have reached the point, says Strauss, when they recognize that "the problems of youth today and the conditions of their childhoods have reached the point where they are unacceptable."[4]

This parental and societal concern has introduced a sense of collective esteem on the part of today's teens, he says. They are coming of age when it is "in" to be a team player for upright causes.

The Millennials' collective esteem is arising when there is a notable absence of heroes for young people to emulate. The absence of heroes, Strauss asserts, will spur this generation to answer the call to heroism and emerge as the next heroes. "We will look so hard for heroes, they [the Millennials] will find that path," he says. "Around 2005, the mood will shift. The Millennials will come of age and attack global problems with ferocity. As we are protecting our children we are forging a sense of community and allowing for the opportunity for peer pressure to become positive. They themselves will clean up the youth culture."

Strauss's premise (and it is only a premise) has been supported by independent studies about this teen generation. The Horatio Alger Association of Distinguished Americans, in a 1996 survey, revealed that among teens' "greatest concerns" is the "decline in moral and social values."[5] The teens profiled in the 1995-1996 edition of *Who's Who Among American High School Students* listed the same thing as their "chief concern" for the first time in the publication's history.

The Higher Education Research Institute survey of college freshmen for the year 1997-1998 reveals that the percentage of college freshmen who think that abortion should be kept legal reached its lowest point since 1979 at 53.5 percent, and those who think there should be laws prohibiting gay relationships rose for the second year in a row to 34 percent. Only 53 percent said they drank beer frequently or occasionally, down from 72 percent in 1981.[6]

The percentage of teens having sex dropped in 1995 for the first time in twenty-five years, according to a National Survey of Family Growth. The study reveals that the percentage of teenage girls having sex had risen from 29 percent in 1970 to 55 percent in 1990 before it dropped to 50 percent in 1995.[7] Teen demonstrators at the 1997 Washington for Jesus march brandished buttons that read "Pet your dog, not your girlfriend" and "Stop your urgin', be a virgin." They prayed for "the strength not to have sex," and so many pledge cards were staked in the mall in Washington, D.C., that they looked like a layer of snow.[8]

Volunteerism is also on the rise among today's teens. A 1996 study conducted by Independent Sector (an organization based in Washington, D.C., that tracks nonprofit activities) shows that in 1995, 13.3 million young people between the ages of twelve and seventeen spent 2.4 billion hours volunteering. That is a 7 percent rise in the number of teens volunteering and a 17 percent increase over the number of hours donated in 1991.[9]

> Teen demonstrators at the 1997 Washington for Jesus march prayed for "the strength not to have sex," and so many pledge cards were staked in the mall in Washington, D.C., that they looked like a layer of snow.

Another positive trend is reflected in a Time/CNN poll taken in late 1997 that revealed "a startling number of youngsters [ages twelve to seventeen], black and white, who seem to have moved beyond their parents' views of race."[10] The youth survey indicates that race was less important to them, on personal and social levels, than it is for adults. "More than half of both white kids and black still consider racism 'a big problem' in America—however, more than a third classify it as 'a small problem.' " When asked how racism affects their own lives, "a startling 89 percent of black teens call it a 'small problem' or 'not a problem at all.' " Beyond that, twice as many black teens as whites said that "failure to take advantage of available opportunities" was a bigger problem for black youth than discrimination. (Only a quarter of black teens said they had been victims of race discrimination, while half of adult blacks said they had been.) "Today's teens," the author writes, "have respect for the past [and] faith in the future."[11]

"Young Americans are changing in the direction of temperance," writes David B. Wolfe in *American Demographics*.[12] All of this reflects what Wolfe calls a "massive unprecedented shift" in the "psychological center of gravity." The decreasing crime rates, the lowering of divorce rates, and the rise in the rate of marriages and "the suddenness and scope" of these changes, Wolfe says, "signal a massive shift in cultural values and personal behavior."[13] "Young adults may dye their hair green and pierce their noses to shock their parents. But at the same time, millions of them attend church weekly and make regular contributions to a retirement fund."[14]

I asked a group of approximately one hundred church-going teens what they thought about the notion that they could be viewed as "heroes." Is this something they want? Here is a sampling of their answers:

"Yes. It gives us hope."

"No. Not all of us are going to be 'good heroes.' "

"Yes. I want to make a difference in the world."

"No. I don't see how I could be a 'hero' to anybody."

"Yes. We definitely have the potential."

"No. We have no sense of guidance."

"Yes. I would like to have an impact on someone's life."

"Oh, noooo. We're self-centered. Don't look at us."

"Yes. It gives us hope that some people believe in us."

"No. It sucks."

"Yes. I just hope we can really be heroes."

"No. Our generation is misled. Heroes fail."

"Yes. It's cool someone thinks positive about us after all the negative we hear."

"No. We're too confused at what's going on around here."

"Yes. But it's a huge responsibility."

"Yes. It makes us seem like we're strong enough to overcome the negative influences in our lives."

"Yes. I hope it doesn't go to our heads!"[15]

Then I asked them to name those whom they look upon as heroes. Counting up all those they cited, their responses were as follows: Jesus edged out the youth pastor twenty citations to eighteen; parents came in third with twelve ("Mom" got an additional eight on her own; "Dad" got an additional five); Michael Jordan was cited eight times; God, seven; martyred missionary Jim Elliot had six; "friends," teachers and grandparents each came away with four; Billy Graham received three citations, while nineteenth-century evangelist Charles Finney and Elisabeth Elliot (Jim Elliot's wife) each took two. Mentioned only once were the apostle Paul, martyred Christians, godly drummers, Job, the deceased musical artist Keith Green, author Joni Eareckson Tada, the Bulls, Martin Luther, Bob Dylan, Beat-generation writer Jack Kerouac, the late basketball star Pete Maravich and Mary (Jesus' mother).

Whether or not they *want* to be the next heroes, my informal survey reveals that they have a clear understanding of what "heroism" implies. Only one out of the hundred or so teens answered, "I don't believe in heroes."

"You watch," says William Strauss. "At the turn of the millennium magazine covers will be proclaiming that they are a wonderful generation—not so much for who they are but for who the nation wants them to be."[16]

But where this generation parts company with Bob Dole's generation is in the cultural environment that has shaped them. The constancy, speed and shock levels of so much of the world they inhabit have honed them to operate in similar extremes, boldly and unabashedly. Moral ambiguity has spurred them to want decisive boundaries and real answers. Spiritual longing has made them ready to give it everything they've got in their quest for God. In other words, they will do things *in the extreme.* When they answer the call to heroism, they will answer it boldly. When it comes to embracing moral truth, they will do so unabashedly. When they give their lives to the Lord, they will serve with everything on the line. An article for *CCM* magazine quotes my description of recording artist Rebecca St. James's success in inspiring and connecting with teens today: "She goes beyond this 'Jesus can save' presentation. She adds, 'Jesus can save, but [he] wants everything you've got.' "[17]

The time is right for parents and the church to seize this season of spiritual ripeness in young people, to capture their longings, win their allegiance, and equip them to give it everything they've got to carry the "extreme gospel" into the next millennium.

Presented below are three examples of church ministries that are breaking new ground. They "do church" in a way that has shown an understanding of and has adapted to the contradictory aspects of today's youth while appropriating their "extremes" to a biblical expression of living faith. These models affirm what Jim Burns, president of the National Institute of Youth Ministry, expresses when he says that "when it comes to today's young people, I believe they are truly motivated to be leaders. And whether churches like it or not, they better train them or lose them."[18]

These models include peer ministry, the "practices," and platoons and shepherds.

Peer Ministry

Mark Senter, a professor at Trinity Evangelical Divinity School, proposes what he thinks should be a new strategy for churches hiring youth ministers. Hire them as if they were church planters, he said, "with the primary objective of developing a team of spiritually mature young adults to start a new church."[19] The vision and trajectory of youth ministry would aim at long-term maturity and the discovery and implementation of spiritual gifts for leadership, and thus avoid the temptation to get them to come by offering attractions of an entertainment-type variety.

This approach has been fleshed out by a "youth church" called

Souled Out, in Mount Prospect, Illinois, founded by Ed Basler and his wife, Cathi.[20]

"We are about real teens meeting a real God," said Ed (who was wearing boots, a leather vest and a bandanna on his head) from the podium at one of the Thursday-evening services. "If you're here for 'religion,' you're not going to find it," he said to the crowd of over a hundred teens seated on the floor around him.

When the Baslers' kids were teens, they always opened their home to their peers and didn't "freak out" if one of the young people was smoking. They spoke openly and freely about God's love for them and always welcomed them. "Before we knew it," says Ed, "we had sometimes eighty kids in our home on a given evening." That was when thoughts of starting a "youth church" began to take shape.

In 1994 the Baslers saw peer ministry modeled elsewhere and "for the first time we saw the truth of *kids ministering to kids,*" says Cathi. "You could see life spring up in these kids."

Inspired by this approach, the Baslers launched Souled Out in December of the same year, meeting in the basement of a local church. In the years since then the ministry has flourished. In 1996 they purchased their present building, which accommodates their multi-faceted menu of activities on almost every night of the week.

The main event is the Thursday-evening outreach service, which sometimes draws crowds of up to three hundred. On Friday and Saturday nights the building is converted into the Heart and Soul Café, offering live music, cafe latte and concerts. On Sunday evenings the ministry holds its Get Real service for mature believers longing for spiritual growth. On Tuesday nights intensive Bible studies (for girls and guys separately) meet in homes. Souled Out also works with area high schools and after-care programs for youths coming out of drug rehab. During any given week, five hundred to seven hundred young people will come through Souled Out's doors.

On a typical Thursday evening a youth band, enveloped in smoke and lasers, leads a time of worship with "alternative"-type worship songs. Ed (in biker garb) reads announcements, and a drama team enacts a modern parable. Video clips are sometimes used to create a mindset for receiving the upcoming message—like the one I saw that had a negative-image Marilyn Monroe look-alike whispering, "In a perfect world there is no word for cheater; in a perfect world there is no word for liar; in a perfect world your parents don't fight."

The "boot" is passed—a cowboy boot in which the offering is received. Then the main speaker, a teen, takes to the mike and offers a testimonial. "A 'perfect world' is not where I come from," a high-school senior said. "I hated my life. I had so many masks that I preferred to lie than to tell the truth. I had two- and three-week depressions when I would just sit in my room and watch bad videos.

"But God was standing next to me the whole time, saying, 'I'm just waiting for you to turn to me.' God is faithful," he said. "He is there for you 24/7."

When the speaker finishes and the service closes with prayer and singing, the ministry begins. Those who were touched or are broken cry and ask for prayer. Young people ministering to their peers put their arms around their hurting brothers and sisters and spend as much time as they need in prayer and ministry.

There is a lot of brokenness in this crowd, and Souled Out taps into it with their no-holds-barred approach, orchestrated by twelve student leaders and their eight adult leaders. The student leaders meet twice a month to study the Bible, receive leadership training and brainstorm about ministry ideas. The adult leaders (two of whom are ordained) meet monthly to oversee the general direction of the ministry. But the teens themselves run the services and carry out behind-the-scenes duties like updating mailing lists and sending out fliers.

One student leader named David, nineteen, says that Souled Out changed "everything" about his life. "I used to be very depressed. The music I listened to was all about suicide and that God was dead. When I came to Souled Out I saw how they had something real with God. I wanted it too."[21]

He helps lead the Tuesday-night "guys" Bible study, and keeping a vigilant eye out on Thursday nights for "where God is working," he welcomes newcomers or prays for people who express needs. He also works with the video ministry, collaborating with other teens to write and produce their own videotaped skits for Thursday nights.

"God is totally using me," he says. "I'm like, thank you, God."

Souled Out's innovative approach, on one level, has made it difficult for some who have grown into young adulthood to settle into a conventional church environment. Says Ed Basler, "This culture is so different from the adult culture. Souled Out has spoiled them for the ordinary." Beyond this, being a "youth church" by definition precludes the development of healthy intergenerational relationships within the congregation. Older people (like the aging boomers, if you can believe it) don't feel comfortable worshiping in that kind of environment, and with those who want to become involved, the Baslers are very cautious. "It is very hard to find an adult who will *commit*. Most of them don't last. And these kids don't need another short-term relationship. They are looking for that mother or father figure."

For all the negatives, however, the peer ministry model—teens themselves doing ministry—excites young people's passion and taps into their leadership potential. Worshipers let down their defenses and pray for (and find) healing and deliverance in an atmosphere of trust and affirmation, free of judgmentalism. Young people who might not otherwise darken the door of a conventional church find a home at Souled Out, where the gospel is presented in its rawest sense and where they relate and find release.

"There is a whole generation that the church has lost," says Ed Basler. "MTV has captured them, but the church hasn't. So we're focusing on teens because most people aren't."

The "Practices"

On the other end of the spectrum is a model that celebrates the "traditional" church while finding creative ways of integrating young people into its conventions. "Christians can learn something from our Jewish and Christian brothers and sisters—and from our own heritage really—that brings people together intergenerationally," says Greg Jones,[22] who presently serves as dean of Duke Divinity School but who formerly served as the "unofficial" associate pastor of Arbutus United Methodist Church in Baltimore, Maryland, where his wife, Susan, served as pastor.

The confirmation process, as the Joneses designed it for their church, drew upon the Jewish tradition of bar mitzvah and the Christian catechesis. The bar mitzvah (and more recently, the bat mitzvah for girls) represents the milestone in the life of a Jewish child climaxing years of preparation during which the child is exposed to Hebrew, the history of Jewish tradition and the Scriptures. During the ceremony, the child leads a substantial portion of the liturgy, which includes prayers (in Hebrew), the reading of psalms, and chants from the Torah

> **"There is a whole generation that the church has lost," says Ed Basler. "MTV has captured them, but the church hasn't. So we're focusing on teens because most people aren't."**

and the Prophets. He or she finishes the service with a bar/bat mitzvah speech sharing what the Scriptures mean to his or her life. Gifts, food and folk dancing are the worshiping community's joyous response to the young person's rite of passage.

In other words, the service provides a meaningful ritual whereby the young person is expected to master the "practices" and rites of community and commit himself or herself to the faith as an adult member. The Joneses modeled their confirmation process after both the bar/bat mitzvah rite-of-passage model and the fourth-century church's tradition of catechesis, or training and discipleship with adult members.

At their church the "training" process involved a six-month period of preparation, beginning in January. Each confirmand was assigned a lay adult mentor who took the child under his or her wing for fellowship and spiritual inquiry. Mentors would attend the confirmation classes with the confirmands and often included the young people when they engaged in their other church responsibilities (like missions meetings). This made a connection between those who were well established in the faith and those who needed to be nurtured in it; the goal was to encourage young people to "lay claim to their own gifts," says Jones.

The confirmation ceremony was held on Pentecost Sunday and treated as an occasion of great festivity. The young people were the liturgists for the day, and their individual written affirmations of faith (part of the confirmation process) were read during the service. The church held a party afterward. Confirmation became, explains Greg Jones, a "rite of passage that says something about the kingdom of God."

The mentors were drawn from a pool of lay adults who had previously actively participated in Covenant Discipleship Groups and who had answered and signed a questionnaire about sexual misconduct issues (a legal necessity for adults who want to work with youth, says Jones).

The discipleship groups were modeled on John Wesley's "class meetings," gathering weekly to examine private devotion, worship, acts of service (like taking a casserole to a sick neighbor) and acts of justice more globally.

The same model was then adapted for the youth after confirmation. The assumption was that the young people would continue in these groups as they got older and would eventually be assimilated into the adult groups.

Jones says the combination of preconfirmation mentoring and the postconfirmation discipleship groups eliminated the confirmation-fallout syndrome that plagues mainline denominations. "You've probably heard that the best way to ensure that kids never come back to church is to confirm them," says Jones. "That has not been the case with us."

The Joneses' church also integrated young participants into many aspects of their worship services, sometimes as lay readers of Scripture, ushers or musicians. All of these "practices," as Greg Jones calls them, are "woven into the tradition of the historical church that needs to be reclaimed today. *Doing things* has been at the heart of the Jewish and Christian faith. The power of the 'practices' is their longevity," he says.

"Sometimes when they read the Scripture they don't do a great job at reading," he says. "But their involvement says to them, 'This is your church too.'"

Platoons and Shepherds

Somewhere in between the peer ministry and "practices" models is the two-pronged platoons and shepherds approach that Shadow Mountain Community Church, in El Cajon, California, has pioneered. This model captures the peer ministry impulse while embracing the intergenerational connection of youth to the larger worshiping body.

After a season of prayer, personal investigation and discussion with other leaders at the church, high-school pastor John Ruhlman began to see that the key to successful ministry (to teens and others) is rooted in Jesus' own model: "Take twelve; graduate eleven; focus on three."[23]

> All of these "practices," as Greg Jones calls them, are "woven into the tradition of the historical church that needs to be reclaimed today. *Doing things* has been at the heart of the Jewish and Christian faith. The power of the 'practices' is their longevity," he says.

He and his colleagues attempted, twice, to launch a small-group approach to their youth program. Twice it failed.

"We prayed a ton about it," he said. After a retreat with the youth ministry staff and about forty youth leaders, it dawned on them that the missing element in their approach to the small-group context was *student leadership*.

Ruhlman immediately set up a new program under the cell group model, only this time with teen leaders. Each group is called a "platoon" and has a student leader. Each platoon leader has a "coach" (an adult mentor) who meets with him or her for an hour or two every week and who also attends the platoon meetings.

Five things must happen at every platoon meeting.

1. Fresh bread. "God has been baking something in your oven this week. What is it?" The participants in the group (which include seven or more regulars and usually two or three newcomers) share Bible passages that have had significant meaning for them during the week. "This is positive reinforcement for a daily Bible study," says Ruhlman. It also encourages newcomers to open their Bibles and start reading.

2. The empty chair. Each platoon always leaves a chair—"the best chair"—empty as a constant visual reminder of the missing friend who needs to be cared for and should be sitting there. The chair reminds the group to pray for these friends, and "almost every week one or two of the people they've prayed for will show up," says Ruhlman. "When that door opens, they are so warmly embraced by the whole group. That is the opposite of what the culture offers these kids. God answers those prayers."

> **Each platoon always leaves a chair—"the best chair"—empty as a constant visual reminder of the missing friend who needs to be cared for and should be sitting there.**

3. Announcements. Mundane as it sounds, this is a critical element in preserving the cohesiveness of the larger youth group. The establishment of forty-some platoons fragmented the larger group, which nevertheless continues to worship together every Sunday (before the regular worship service) and holds monthly outreach events for unreached friends. All of these meetings are highlighted through the announcements, preserving the connectedness of each platoon to the larger group.

4. Lesson. The student platoon leader "gets into the Word."

5. Prayer, care, share. In "platoon notebooks" published by the church, platoon leaders record praise items or struggles and needs shared in the context of this prayer time. The group prays together; then the platoon leader revisits the needs mentioned the week earlier, which sets a tone of nurture and follow-up in the group and teaches the student leaders pastoral shepherding skills.

One platoon leader, named David (seventeen), says that it wasn't until he assumed this leadership role that his faith became a truly vital force in his life, "I knew a lot about the Bible, but I never really felt capable of being a leader until I started doing it. Then I thought, *I can do this.* So I decided I was through with this halfhearted stuff and that I was going to be sold out. I started reading the Bible and that made me stop thinking about myself all the time. It made me start caring about others. Being a platoon leader is the best thing that has happened to me."[24]

Another leader, named Kendra (seventeen), says, "It's encouraged me to know I'm needed—it's not a pride thing. It's just seeing how the Lord can use anyone."[25]

All of the platoons gather together on Sunday mornings for corporate worship that includes singing contemporary songs, watching videos and hearing a message from Ruhlman. After that service the teens join the larger congregation for the conventional worship service.

But youth ministry at Shadow Mountain does not stop with the platoons and the large group activities. To integrate the teens of the church with the adult members, Wayne Rice—who founded Youth Specialties, is the director of Understanding Your Teenager and also happens to attend Shadow Mountain, where he works with Ruhlman—has launched a mentoring program. His motto: "Every student with a shepherd."[26] Rice has undertaken a training program in which he works with adult volunteers, training them to be mentors to the youth in the church. "Our kids don't have any significant adults in their lives; some of them don't even have parents."

Successful mentoring is a struggle, says Rice, because "most people are too busy and don't have time for other people's kids. But that is why our kids are in trouble today. No one has time for them anymore."

It can also "get weird," he says, because mentoring also means that the adult volunteers will get fingerprinted and be cross-checked on the FBI database of pedophiles. "Rather than have it be this negative thing, we make it a celebration, proclaiming, 'we're above reproach,' " says Ruhlman. "We make a ceremony out of it."

The mentoring program remains independent of the platoons but the two programs have overlapped well. Many of the adults who have undergone Rice's training have ended up as platoon coaches. And Ruhlman gives Rice the names of young people in the youth group who are in special need of adult relationships, particularly teens without a father or mother (or both).

Ruhlman says that there have been five grandparents serving as platoon coaches and fourteen parents who have coached their own kids. "People have come up to me and said, 'John, what's going on? My kid wants me to disciple him!' "

Key Points

☐ For all the extremes in youth culture today, one of the most notable and seemingly contradictory extreme is their being hailed as the next generation of heroes.

☐ I asked a hundred teens who their heroes were. Jesus took pride of place. Their youth leader came in second, their parents third. Michael Jordan took fourth.

☐ When and if the Millennials answer the call, they will answer it boldly.

☐ Empowering young people by giving them leadership roles in church ministries, including serving their peers, has magnified the relevance and impact of church in their lives.

☐ Traditional ritual within worship has kept history alive for young people and sets church apart from their electronically stimulated world.

☐ Young people respond to accountability groups and mentoring relationships, though there is an inadequate number of committed adults who are willing to lead them.

Prayer Point

Lord, thank you for raising up a generation of young people who are courageous and bold. Your church needs their creativity and leadership. Help us to love your church and to be worthy teachers and guides in training our youth to be its next generation of leaders.

6

Does God
Have a Face?

C hurch was late in getting started that steamy Saturday evening in late May. Three of the six teenagers running "the
service" hadn't yet arrived when it was set to begin at 7:45
p.m. Romane, we knew, wasn't coming. He had a track meet down-
state. (He said he would "be with us in spirit.") The other two, however,
were integral. Vanessa was in charge of the testimony time and James
had volunteered "to bring the Word."

Honestly, though, it wasn't as if we had hordes of people shuffling
restlessly waiting to begin. Only a few had shown up to participate in
this experiment. Mary, who was in charge of the worship songs, came
with her mother; she was using the extra time to scribble the words out
on poster board with a magic marker. Donny brought his mother and
little brother. He was going to lead us in a Spanish worship song and
was going to "proclaim" (read) the Word; he used the lull to practice
reading his passage out loud. Tony had corralled a coterie of his youth
group buddies who were using the time (when they weren't roaring
around outside) to roll a carpet onto the cement floor and set up the
folding table that would be the altar. Tony was in charge of extending
the welcome and prayer of invocation and would do so when I gave

him the signal to start. My husband, a pastor, came too; he was the designated "pastoral presence." So we were few in number.

James finally arrived around 8:00 p.m., harried and with blue lips (from cotton candy—he had spent the day at Great America, a local amusement park). He asked frenetically if I had a Bible.

A Bible?

Only Donny had remembered to bring his Bible. He had finished practicing his passage, so he handed it to James, who then sequestered himself for a few minutes of intense preparation for his message.

Mary had finished writing out the words to the songs and had clamped them to an easel up front, Tony's friends had pulled out folding chairs for the two mothers, and my husband sat with the youth group rowdies on the floor. Vanessa still hadn't arrived, so Mary and I started improvising how to do the testimony time.

Not wanting to aggravate those who, first of all, had come and, second of all, had shown up on time, we decided—ready or not—to let the experiment begin.

Tony, in shorts, a T-shirt and flip-flops, ambled to the front and stood before the "altar." He fidgeted. Facing his peers, the moms, Pastor Bob and me—all of whom sat in a semicircle around him—he welcomed us and thanked us for coming. Then he prayed, "Lord, may your Holy Spirit come down on us."

We had gathered in an attempt to "do church" as an outgrowth of an all-day forum that the teens and I had shared two days earlier. During the forum we listened to the 1995 song "One of Us," performed by Joan Osborne, that asks the question "If God had a face, what would it look like?"[1] The song poses the question that we attempted to answer both in the forum and during our "church" experiment. We concluded that the answer to her question was yes, God does have a face, and he's left it to his church to reveal it. (As Mary put it, "The church is the only reminder left on earth that Christ was here.") So our challenge in the forum was, first, to examine the notion of "church" as it is portrayed in several biblical references and, second, to find a way to interface those portrayals with the cultural realities and peculiarities that teens today bring to their worldview. In other words, how can we create a "face" for God that people will "see"?

> "The church is the only reminder left on earth that Christ was here."—MARY

In the course of our day together we were not attempting to answer the questions of all the ages about the nature of the bride of Christ in her visible and invisible expressions. These young people, though raised in the church, are not biblical exegetes. Biblical scholars may cringe at the off-the-cuff interpretations of passages, and theologians may squirm at the imprecision of thought and application. But no one will doubt both the commitment and the startling ferocity with which these youth defended their commitment to be true to the gospel.

Before probing the biblical material, I asked the young people to offer their definitions of "church."

"A place where Christians can come together to worship God," said Tony.

"The church is a family. It's somewhere we can fall down on our knees and repent for our sins," said Vanessa.

Mary said it is a place "where we can come knowing that we are weak, where we can encourage one another" and "receive his strength through prayer and Communion."

> "The church is a family. It's somewhere we can fall down on our knees and repent for our sins."—VANESSA

Donny said it is "a building of concrete, brick and wood" where people "worship God" and come for "prayer and a biblical message" and where "God gives us our duties for the week."

Romane said it is "where people go who believe that Jesus died on the cross for their sin."

James summed it up: "God's people gathered around God's Word declaring God's glory."

To test their definitions we probed some biblical passages: "And I tell you that you are Peter, and on this rock I will build my church, and the gates of Hades will not overcome it" (Matthew 16:18 NIV). This is the first of only two times in the gospels that the Greek word *ekklēsia* (the called-out ones) is used of the church (the other is Matthew 18:17). I asked them what they thought Jesus meant when he said

> Church is "a building of concrete, brick and wood" where people "worship God" and come for "prayer and biblical message" and where "God gives us our duties for the week."—DONNY

those words, and their answers were as different as their personalities.

Vanessa and Romane saw the verse as a promise of protection. Vanessa said, "We're safe in the church with his presence around us," and Romane, "God is protecting us against the devil. So you're safe—which is hard to believe sometimes."

James saw the verse as an affirmation of the doctrine of election: "We're chosen by God. The gates of Hades are not strong enough to overcome the people he has chosen."

For Mary the verse was a mandate: "We have a mission to this world that he has given us."

Tony remarked that Jesus simply "meant it for Peter."

But beyond these general descriptions, the teens concluded that our mission also includes discerning what being the "church" means

> "God is protecting us against the devil. So you're safe [in church]—which is hard to believe sometimes."—ROMANE

in terms of the time/space gathering of believers. From these "popcorn verses" (as James called them at one point) the teens culled their ideas about what "church" means in a given time and cultural context.

First Peter 2:5 (read by James): "You also, like living stones, are being built into a spiritual house to be a holy priesthood, offering spiritual sacrifices acceptable to God through Jesus Christ" (NIV).

First Kings 8:10-12 (read by Tony): "When the priests withdrew from the Holy Place, the cloud filled the temple of the LORD. And the priests could not perform their service because of the cloud, for the glory of the LORD filled his temple. Then Solomon said, 'The LORD has said that he would dwell in a dark cloud' " (NIV).

Ephesians 2:19-22 (read by Vanessa from her King James Version of the Bible): "Now therefore ye are no more strangers and foreigners, but fellow-citizens with the saints, and of the household of God; and are built upon the foundation of the apostles and prophets, Jesus Christ himself being the chief corner stone; in whom all the building fitly framed together groweth unto an holy temple in the Lord: in whom ye also are builded together for an habitation of God through the Spirit."

Praise and Worship

The "spiritual house" reference in 1 Peter prompted James to conclude that unlike the temple in the Old Testament, "the spiritual house" today "is formed by these living stones"—God's people. "Flat out, if I had to cut out all the other words, I would say [the church] is God's people. The people of God are God's church."

The reference from 1 Kings, in which the glory of the Lord fills the temple, inspired the group to conclude that for the "living stones" (God's people) to fill the "spiritual temple" with "the glory of the Lord," the gathered believers have to manifest, as Tony succinctly put it, "praise and worship."

This does not mean that worship should be entertaining, said Mary. "Worship is not entertainment" or "a place for people to share their talents—or what they *think* their talents are."

Mary's comment prompted the conversation to segue into a discussion about what worship is.

"People need to be active in worship," said Donny. "The church is supposed to get people from the audience active in what you're doing instead of just people that are on stage or up front."

Tony concurred, "I like to clap and move around. I just have to get up and move." James said he gets frustrated when people request songs that "get them jumping up and down and clapping. I'm not saying that's bad, but some of these songs mean absolutely nothing; they have no worth words-wise. You're not lifting anything up to God when you do that; you're having a good time, and we don't want people coming to Christ because they're having a good time."

Vanessa, prefacing her comments with the proviso "We may plan an order of service, but the Holy Ghost may step in and change the order," said that praise and worship consists of "people who are holy praising his holy name for his many blessings."

Most agreed that music was an integral part of worship. "Music is a way we can give praise to God," said Mary. "It's active and God-centered."

James conceded that "good time" or not, "church" should include "psalms, hymns and spiritual songs."

Romane's was the lone voice that asserted that praise through song was optional, "We don't need all the songs, even though I love them and want them. (Believe me, those keep it interesting.)"

So the consensus was to begin "praise and worship" with song, despite James's squeamishness about clapping.

Keeping with their conviction that worship should be active, Vanessa suggested that during our "church" experiment testimonies should be included in "praise and worship." She said she would lead off by sharing her own testimony and then open it up to anyone else who might want to share.

Mary added that "taking an offering is a kind of worship too."

From our discussion the group concluded that "praise and worship" should be active, have coherence and value "words-wise," be God-centered, and not necessarily be a "good time."

Mary asked us to stand as she led us in the opening songs. Ronnie, one of the youth-group guys Tony brought, accompanied us on the guitar as we stumbled through the first song. (Mary is tender-hearted and so did not whip the congregation into shape when they sang weakly. The guys mumbled and the moms were tentative.) If the first song limped along, the next one bolted. That is because this one was the Spanish song—Donny's brainchild—called "Alabaré" ("I will praise"). He read the phrases in Spanish, then translated them into English so the non-Spanish speakers would know what they were singing. Latino worship—even without guitar and, in this case, with only Donny and his family members setting the pace—has an effervescent quality that energizes singing. Even the youth-group guys got into this one.

Vanessa was slotted to lead us in the next song. But like she said, you can plan the order of a service but the Holy Ghost might step in and change it. So we moved on to the final song, which Ronnie knew and which flowed easily.

After the singing, Mary stepped in for Vanessa to lead the testimony time. One mom shared about an all-night prayer vigil her church had sponsored in preparation for the coming of a new pastor, and James told about a young man whom he had been "praying for since sixth grade" who finally found the Lord. "It challenged me to be more bold about my faith," he said.

Mary then moved us into the offering. Ronnie improvised on the guitar while the basket made its way around for the offering. (Romane had suggested that we take a "love offering" for the owner of the studio we were using for our service. "By taking up a collection we're going to say, 'Thank you. God bless you. We appreciate it.' ")

With the "praise and worship" portion of the service concluded, Mary deferred to Donny, who introduced the next aspect of what the teens said church had to include: "proclamation of the Word."

Proclamation of the Word

The "popcorn" verses from which the teens derived their understanding of the proclamation of the Word included:

☐ John 8:31-32 (read by Mary): "To the Jews who had believed him, Jesus said, 'If you hold to my teaching, you are really my disciples. Then you will know the truth, and the truth will set you free'" (NIV).

☐ Second John 9 (read by Vanessa): "Whosoever transgresseth, and abideth not in the doctrine of Christ, hath not God. He that abideth in the doctrine of Christ, he hath both the Father and the Son" (KJV).

The Word of God loomed large in the teens' minds as a critical, nonnegotiable component that must be at the center of any gathering of the people of God. Donny said that the church had to have a "biblical message."

Tony said that a church must "be devoted—like in Acts 2—and always have a lesson that is based on biblical truths." He was referring to Acts 2:42: "They devoted themselves to the apostles' teaching and to the fellowship, to the breaking of bread and to prayer" (NIV).

James added, "If you're followers of God, then you're followers of his Word. That's got to be central."

Vanessa said, "Scripture might have something to lead you along the path that God is trying to lead you on."

So the Word, without exception, has to be integral. The question of how to appropriate it at the church level introduced a many-faceted exploration. "I think a lot of people hate to read the Bible because it changes them sometimes," said Romane. "A lot of people get upset

> A church must "be devoted—like in Acts 2—and always have a lesson that is based on biblical truths."—TONY

when they read it because they find out what they're doing is wrong and they don't want to know it's wrong. Once a Sunday-school teacher or the pastor or you yourself read a verse like that, ain't no use going up to God and saying 'I didn't know.'"

Added Vanessa, "We have to interpret the Word correctly to receive the truth, to spread the news."

"We have to accept his teaching," added Mary, "and live our lives based on that."

"Not just teaching," interjected James. "But teaching of truth. The only way we know what's true is if God says it's true."

"That's why people should go to church and Sunday school," said Romane. "A lot of people say that they believe in God but they don't go to church. I believe the reason we go to church and Sunday school is because we have the pastor and Sunday-school teachers who give you the correct meaning of what's in the Bible. A pastor, I'm sure in most cases, knows more about it than the average person. That's a good reason to go to church, because you'll learn the truth. The Word can still be misinterpreted, but there is less chance of that happening."

From this conversation it seemed apparent that the Word of God is to function on a number of levels. Romane mentioned the effect of simply "reading" the Word: "It changes them sometimes"; and Vanessa indicated that the Scripture "might lead you." This suggests that, in their understanding, the Scriptures have power in and of themselves and so the service should include the simple reading of a biblical passage without commentary. Because of the Word's ability to "change" and "lead" it was also suggested that prayer follow the reading of the uninterpreted Word. Said Mary, "Prayer is where he's really empowering us. That's when he's allowed to work through us. We have to give him that."

The teens mentioned another aspect of the Word: teaching—true teaching, which, Romane said, is "a good reason" people should go to church.

To fulfill all aspects of the "proclamation of the Word," then, the teens included reading the uninterpreted Word, prayer in response, and teaching of the Word.

Donny volunteered to read the uninterpreted "proclamation." James said he'd "be comfortable teaching the Word or leading prayer" so the group deferred to his leadership for both. Romane thought maybe we should "just have an altar call as a prayer" and someone else thought that only one person should pray. But Mary objected, "If you want to be relevant to this generation then I think we should have interactive prayer. People feel that if they're not just seeing someone else up there doing it then it means a lot more. They're actually involved with it."

"Now I'm going to read Psalm 41," Donny said with projection and confidence (except he was really going to read Psalm 91—but no one caught it). He read slowly in a measured voice. No baseball caps were removed during the proclamation of the Word, but all eyes in the semicircle of young people were fixed intently on the reader.

A thousand may fall at your side, ten thousand at your right hand, but it will not come near you. . . .

You will tread upon the lion and the cobra; you will trample the great lion and the serpent. . . .

"Because he loves me," says the LORD, "I will rescue him; I will protect him, for he acknowledges my name." (NIV)

"Praise God," said one of the moms.

Donny finished reading Psalm 91, then closed his Bible and passed it off to James, who came forward to sit in the folding chair up front. With his blue cap and blue lips, rubbing his palms and with elbows on knees, James said, "We're going to pray.

"Prayer is the most work of anything because it requires so much concentration," he said.

"When someone else is praying, be amen-ing the words to God.

"I know we're all supposed to have short attention spans and all that, but we're going to spend some time in prayer. It's a heck of a lot of work. We're going to pray through topics."

James then led us in a series of prayer "topics," and the first focused on "praising God for who he is."

"You are holy, holy, holy," James said. "Thank you for your forgiveness which is infinite beyond the scope of thought or imagination."

Others were "amening" and adding short sentence prayers:

"Thank you for your love and mercy."

"Thank you for your friendship."

"Every knee shall bow. You are powerful, the one true almighty God."

"Everything we worry about, you work it out in your own time."

In time, after we praised God for who he is, James led us into a quiet time to *think about* who he is. A pregnant pause followed.

After this time of silence James introduced the next topic: "confronting our sinfulness" and "confessing our unworthiness."

"We are sinful, sinful," James said. "We don't allow your Word to soften our hearts. We are hard-hearted. We don't seize those opportunities you bring us to share your truth; help us not to be ashamed.

"Forgive us for being hypocrites," he said. "We go to church for all the wrong reasons. Sometimes we don't learn that we can be saved from hell and from our sin natures. What expression can we have except gratitude? And we don't even do that."

The sound of the spinning fans lent a sense of being suspended in time without cognizance of the silence that followed James's corporate confession. In due course, after the silence had lingered, he led us into the final topic of prayer: "general requests." Someone prayed for the church that was receiving a new pastor (mentioned during the testimony time), and others lifted more sentence prayers. When these were exhausted, someone closed with the words "Thank you that you hear our prayers with a kind heart."

And then James opened the Bible: "This is God's Word."

> Whatever happens, conduct yourselves in a manner worthy of the gospel of Christ. Then, whether I come and see you or only hear about you in my absence, I will know that you stand firm in one spirit, contending as one man for the faith of the gospel without being frightened in any way by those who oppose you. This is a sign to them that they will be destroyed, but that you will be saved—and that by God. For it has been granted to you on behalf of Christ not only to believe on him, but also to suffer for him, since you are going through the same struggle you saw I had, and now hear that I still have. (Philippians 1:27-30 NIV)

"This is a great passage," James began. All heads were turned toward and eyes focused on him. "Something that sticks in my mind is when Paul says to 'conduct yourselves in a manner worthy of the gospel of Christ.'

"We are pitiful sinners doomed to hell because of our sin natures.

We have more in common with the termites than God does with us because of our sin. We keep turning back to sin. And despite that he loved us so much that he sent his Son to be spit upon and rejected by everyone—even his closest disciples.

"This is the gospel. What a high calling it is: to conduct yourselves in a manner worthy. It's such an awesome gospel. If you're really getting into God's Word you'll know what it is to conduct yourself in a manner that is worthy . . .

"We need to put on the gospel of Christ like a veil over us. Every action we do will be done in light of that. We can't reach it, but we should always be reaching for it . . .

"It says, 'Stand firm as one man.' He wants the church to be unified. So the first step is conducting yourself in a manner worthy of the gospel of Christ. Then we will become like-minded. That will bring about unity—'contending as one man' . . .

"When people see us living in a manner worthy of the gospel of Christ and unified, they will know that you've got it right and that they are doomed; they will know that you are saved by God . . ."

For approximately ten minutes James "brought the Word." With sincere conviction he wove the meaning of one verse of the text into the next, introducing cause and effect where Paul may not have intended it. But exegesis aside, his message was moving us to a new place. He forced us to think about what Paul meant when he said, "Whatever happens, conduct yourselves in a manner worthy of the gospel."

When James concluded his message, he said, "We're going to have the opportunity to take Communion. Communion is about the gospel of Christ."

The Bread and the Cup

"Communion," more than any other issue, took on such a level of importance that discussion of it during the forum nearly derailed the experiment. From his King James Version of the Bible, Romane read the passage we examined relating to the Lord's Supper:

> And he said unto them, "With desire I have desired to eat this passover with you before I suffer: For I say unto you, I will not anymore eat thereof, until it be fulfilled in the kingdom of God." And he took the cup, and gave thanks, and said, "Take this, and divide it among yourselves: For I say unto you, I will not drink of the fruit of the vine, until the kingdom of God shall come."
>
> And he took bread, and gave thanks, and brake it, and gave unto them, saying, "This is my body which is given for you: this do in remembrance of me." Likewise also the cup after supper, saying, "This cup is the new testament in my blood, which is shed for you." (Luke 22:15-20)

The sentiment resounded that the sacraments (including baptism, but for our purposes we focused on the Lord's Supper) were essential to any expression of church. "Christ commanded us to observe it," Mary said. "Once a month is okay, but every week would be better."

Tony said, "At the end of what Jesus said, he always says, 'Do this in remembrance of me.' I think we're supposed to do it until he returns. And this is a way we remember what he did for us, how he shed his blood on the cross and what he had to do to take away our sins."

Vanessa said taking Communion is "like cleansing yourself. . . . When you drink the blood and take his body it, like, cleanses you and makes you a better person for that month, or whatever."

> **"He chose holy Communion as a testimony that when you're actually doing something with your hands, you're tasting something, when it is more than just your thoughts. Your whole body has to get involved with it."—JAMES**

James said, "He chose holy Communion as a testimony that when you're actually doing something with your hands, you're tasting something, when it is more than just your thoughts. Your whole body has to get involved with it. Because we are the created, we don't understand completely why he chose that, but he did. I know when I take Communion it carries weight."

But that "weight" prompted James to raise the question: "Should we even be doing Communion? Do we do things that are designated for a real church instead of a model church?"

Romane countered, "When you say 'real church' you make it sound like we're pretending."

"I don't think we should be taking the rites of the traditional church, the things that have been designated to the power of the church, taking those for ourselves," James said.

"What you're saying is not true," answered Romane. "He [Jesus] didn't say, 'Only the church can do this.' You know what I'm saying? If what you're saying is right, then forming this group is wrong, or youth group is wrong. I mean it says in the Good Book that we can do this. God didn't say who can serve it. We all have traditions and we're trying to say, 'Okay, take tradition and throw it out the window.' "

"I've been taught that it is supposed to be an ordained pastor [who serves]," said Tony.

"My mom and dad would visit people who were either in a hospital or couldn't come to church and give them Communion. And they're not ordained," said Mary.

"The people [in our church] decided that an ordained pastor should do it," interjected Vanessa.

"I'm not trying to argue over nitpicky things," James countered, "[though] there's a lot of nitpicky things I feel uncomfortable with. But it's because of a basic philosophy that I want to make sure we have straight and right. Some traditions are shaped by the Word of God. Some are not. Whenever you're doing something that goes contrary to tradition, that's all right as long as you're very sure that this is what the Word of God teaches. Tradition kind of serves as a buffer, and so I don't think we've studied church enough. I mean, we've done 'popcorn verses,' but we've kind of read them and talked about them, but I don't think we've really chewed on the Word of God."

"I don't think it would be wise for 'just us' to become a 'regular church' without the guidance of someone who was more grounded in really what the church is," Mary said. "It would be kind of foolish for us to try and put together a church without really going into what does the church mean. But I don't think that makes this wrong."

The issue of serving Communion took us back to our initial discussion about the nature of the church. James himself had defined the church, "flat out," as "the people of God." The teens hailed the ideas outlined in 1 Peter 2:5 about the church being a "spiritual house" comprising "living stones" embodying the priesthood of all believers.

So whether or not our small coterie of gathered believers could partake of Communion forced the question of whether our experiment could be considered "real" church or "pretend" church (or whether there could be such a thing as a "pretend" church).

The group felt that the celebration of Communion was fundamental to identifying ourselves as gathered believers and obeying Christ's command to "do this" in his remembrance. Said Mary, "It goes with the idea that we're to worship God with all our hearts and souls and minds—that you're making your body a living temple for him. That it's everything you are that is being given over to him. Eating is so important to us. You do it three times a day or more, and you really depend on it whether it's conscious or not. So that's something he's claimed for his own."

Romane added, "You have to actually do something to show that you are thinking about God instead of just saying you are, or whatever." But he demurred, saying, "If [James] feels uncomfortable with the sacraments, then I don't mind not having it."

Then Mary said, "How 'bout if your husband [meaning my husband, Bob] serves it?"

Quieted by the thought that a member of the ordained clergy, my husband, would administer the elements, James acquiesced. And the discussion then moved to more mundane matters like whether we should serve wine or grape juice (grape juice was chosen in deference to any potential alcoholics who might attend) and leavened or unleavened bread (they settled on saltines). The group opted for a central table to which people would come to partake, rather than having the elements distributed. "It's more like we're all sharing in this bread and puts more of a sense of receiving it individually. That you have to give something up to receive it," said Mary.

James deferred to "Pastor Bob" overseeing Communion as the climax of their service. Casually dressed but dignified in his khakis and loafers, Bob stood behind the table and told a story:

"I heard on the radio once about a man who said, 'See this tie I have on? It's sanctified. See this shirt? And these shoes? They're sanctified.'

"He meant," Bob said, "that these common items had been, essentially, 'chosen' or set apart for a specific purpose.

"In the same way, we're common. We're sinners, as James pointed out. But we've been set apart. These elements for Communion—they're common: grape juice, plastic cups, saltines. However, we're sanctifying them, setting them apart as symbols for the body and blood of Christ. In this sense, the common becomes transsignified. We're to examine our lives before partaking because there is danger if we don't, what is common can bring damnation upon us."

He continued, "God took what is common—human flesh and blood—and used it to win our salvation." Lifting the bread, Bob said, " 'This is my body given for you.' Take. Eat. Feed on him in faith." Lifting the cup, he said, " 'This is my blood shed for you.' Take. Drink the cup of salvation, which he drank to its dregs."

Worshipers lined up in front of the table and, passing the bread and then the cup, individually partook as Bob said quietly, "This is his body. This is his blood." Donny collected the plastic cups as the partakers passed by him to return to their seats.

James had suggested that we close the service singing the hymn "Holy, Holy, Holy." Ronnie didn't know it so we sang it a cappella.

"Holy, holy, holy, Lord God Almighty, all thy works shall praise Thy name. . . .

"Holy, holy, holy. Though the darkness hide thee, though the eye of sinful man thy glory may not see. Only Thou art holy. . . .

"Holy, holy, holy.

"There is none beside thee. Perfect in power, in love, and purity."

What Worship Is

This experiment taught me several things. It showed me that when it comes to public worship, these young people value intimacy and interactivity, tactile expressions and tradition.

Intimacy and interactivity. By including a "sharing time" in "praise and worship" the teens reflected the value they place on relating openly, deeply and with vulnerability to one another. The singing also signaled the importance they place on relationships and interactivity, as the Latino contingent taught us a song from their tradition and the others responded robustly.

The value they place on intimacy and interactivity was also evident in their inclusion of prayer as part of "the proclamation of the Word." In their minds, hearing the Word is intended to evoke a response, and prayer is the expression of that response. Scripture should be read publicly, it should confront them publicly, and they should be compelled to respond publicly in prayer. Prayer is action. All of God's worshiping people, not just the people "up front," are equipped and in fact constrained to pray in accordance with the Spirit's prompting.

Tactile expressions and tradition. The discussion about Communion was most telling in this regard. Both the traditional and the tactile aspects of the sacrament came into play in the discussion. The experiment was almost derailed because of the weight James placed on the Lord's Supper, which arose from his tradition more than from our study of the biblical passages. Only the equally tenacious resolve on the part of others, who insisted that Communion was integral to worship (coupled with the convenient providence that my husband is an ordained clergyman), salvaged the experiment. James also pointed out during the discussion that the visual and ritualistic aspect of the sacrament provides a way for the community of faith to *taste* and to *touch* and to *partake in* the drama of our salvation with parabolic force.

They sang in Spanish, lingered in prayer, thought about who God is and got up out of their seats to partake of the Lord's Supper. Worship was active. It took conscious resolve to get out of their comfort zones, to give something up, to move into new territory—or to put it another way, to get up off their couch-potato behinds and defy the propensity to change the channel. The activity, the intimacy, the touching and tasting, the waiting in prayer, all counteract and contradict the default mechanisms bred into them by their media-saturated culture. Worship and being in the presence of God is not just another consumer option.

They kept their baseball hats on. That could offend some people. They wore shorts, flipflops, T-shirts and—in James's case—blue lips. We ignored these (sometimes shocking) physical accouterments that attend youth culture so as not to create an obstacle to their seeing the face of God in the context of "church."

Donny said that the church is "concrete, brick and wood"—mundane and vulnerable like the baseball caps, the lack of Bibles, the tentative singing, the blue lips, the misidentified psalm. "We are weak," as Mary said.

I learned something else from this experiment. The question arose at one point whether our gathering could be considered "real" church or "pretend" church. When we sang our final song, something happened that answered the question.

"Holy, holy, holy."

The tentativeness and discomfort of singing a cappella began to evaporate. The voices of the moms, the youth-group guys and their siblings, Pastor Bob, and me came together in perfect unison and resounded off the high ceilings. For all our struggling earlier on, there wasn't a missed note this time. The volume and clarity seemed to increase with each verse. "Holy, holy, holy" reverberated clearly and forcefully. It felt as if God himself broke through our frail attempts to take hold of him.

"Holy, holy, holy."

Our feet were firmly planted on concrete, but the Spirit found a way to break through, "pitiful sinners" though we were. He made his presence known.

"Holy, holy, holy" became more than the individual voices reaching for the right note.

We were "transsignifed" into a gathering of the church.

Key Points

☐ The youth in my teen forum see church as a place of protection where they can receive strength and hear God's Word and where they are to get their marching orders for the week.

☐ Worship to them means that everyone is active and involved, not just the "people on stage or up front."

☐ The Word of God is intended to change people. It is up to the church to offer the opportunity for people to respond in prayer, confession, service and accountability.

☐ Communion, in their minds, is fundamental to identifying ourselves as gathered believers; it is obeying Christ's command to "do this" in his remembrance. It is not for pretenders.

☐ The aspects of church that stand out as most important to these young people include intimacy, interactivity, tradition and getting up out of the pew.

Prayer Point

Lord, build your church through these honorable and resolute young people.

7

The Grand Narrative

When I think about Button, my grandmother whom I mentioned in the opening chapter, I don't think of a woman who—as my father put it—"was mostly impressed by the punishing God." She seemed more "impressed" with God's mercy, at least in the letters she wrote to me:

> I am old and getting weary for I just never seem to see any change in the life of some of those I love so dearly. I was so glad to get the picture you sent. Your dad looked so real I felt I had to touch him. And your baby is so sweet and has such beautiful eyes. I could see in your dad's face a happiness no one else but that baby could put there. God will answer. A miracle will happen, you'll see. So let's pray for a miracle.

The miracle that my grandmother was praying for—and that she asked me to pray for—was that her son, my father, would find his way back. Not to Liverpool, which he had left unceremoniously to join the army, but to belief in all those things about God that his mother had taught him in his youth. Somewhere between tipping outhouses and his entrepreneurial enterprise my father "lost his way," as Button once put it to me.

On one occasion during my teen years—after the hubbub of the pool party had given way to the stillness of night—my three sisters and I were awakened out of our sleep by the sound of our parents fighting. I used to go to sleep regularly with the TV running so as to block out any such sounds, but this particular evening the four of us were abruptly aroused and found ourselves in the middle of a family crisis. The prosperity we enjoyed in our youth was darkened by the bondage we all experienced as a result of my father's alcoholism. Hambone Dodge never knew this side of Moon Murray. Moon would not have recognized himself. But my father's alcoholism hung over us like a shroud. We felt powerless in the face of this force that so colored and distorted our lives.

I don't remember the details of that upsetting night, other than that a kind neighbor ended up in our hallway helping us girls throw clothes together so that we could spend the night at her house. I didn't sleep that night. I remember sitting on the bed in a room that was not mine, looking out of the window at our house. There were no lights on.

When I made my way home the following morning, I was not surprised to see a suitcase opened and half-packed on my parents' bed. The only question in my mind was which one was leaving.

I saw my father sitting alone on the couch in the living room.

"Are you leaving?" I asked.

"Do you want me to leave?"

Despite everything, instinctively I said, "No."

My father started to cry. I went to him and hugged him. He looked at me and, with tears falling from his one eye, he said, "I don't want to leave. I have too much to lose."

The rest of that day and the days that followed remain a blur in my memory. My father did not leave. But two things happened in the subsequent weeks that changed everything.

The first thing that happened was that I blew my knee out. Not unlike my father's alcoholism, a floating kneecap that regularly dislocated plagued my life. I was a member of our gymnastic squad and a cheerleader, and I played on the girls' basketball team, all of which served as a meaningful escape for me. But one time when I performed one of my more gutsy experiments on the tumbling mat in our school gym, I landed wrong and came down on my bad knee full force, tearing the ligaments so badly that, as the doctor dryly put it, "There will be no more sports."

I shake my head when I think how those few words could have shattered my world. That loss, coupled with my father's troubles, drove me to despondency. I sat on my bed, my left leg extended straight out in front of me (too swollen to bend), and I began to cry.

That was to be expected, given the circumstances. What was not normal, however, was what happened to me there. One moment I was buckled over in sobs, and the next moment the tears that ran down my cheeks came forth from an uncontainable, strange joy.

Somehow, without my asking and without anyone prompting me to "receive the Lord," he found me on my bed and lifted my face. In a moment he rescued me and began to rewrite the script of my life. I remember looking up "Jesus Christ" in the encyclopedia because I couldn't put my finger on a Bible.

That was February 1972. I was sixteen.

But a second event occurred that also changed everything. About five weeks after my spontaneous conversion, as my mother drove me to the hospital to undergo knee surgery, she turned to me and said, "Your father has quit drinking."

How many times had I heard that before? I was unfazed. I underwent the operation that left me bound to a hospital bed for a week with a cast from my toes to my groin. Upon my return home, however, it became evident that something very different had come over my father. A new friend was calling all the time and visiting frequently. This, I learned, was his "sponsor" from AA—Alcoholics Anonymous. My father was going to meetings every night of the week.

That was April 1972—less than six weeks after my encounter with Jesus Christ. I felt sure that my father's deliverance from alcoholism (he never had another drink from that day until the day he died) was the Lord's way of telling me, *This is real.*

Reversing the Great Reversal

Madeleine L'Engle describes a conversation she had with her son, then age ten, when she read him a portion from an early draft of her book *The Arm of the Starfish.* A character showed up in the narrative whom L'Engle hadn't factored into the original outline. His name was Joshua and he was a Jesus figure. "I was very surprised to see Joshua," she says. When she read the part in which Joshua got shot, her son objected, saying, "Change it."

"I can't change it; that's what happened," she said.

"But you're the writer, you can change it."

"No," she said, "I can't change it. That's what happened."[1]

What L'Engle meant is that there is a force bigger than *what we want* playing itself out in our world. I call it the Grand Narrative. And it seems that in our electronically saturated, consuming world we have lost our place in the unfolding plot. Our senses have grown dull and the consumer mindset has convinced us that *our* narrative is all that matters in the grand scheme of things. We like to think that "the story" is ours to write, and we attempt to advance the plot according to what we think we deserve. "One of the supreme ironies of our age is that the society that has talked and written most about the fulfillment of the self shows the least evidence of it," writes Eugene Peterson. "People obsessed with the cultivation of the self have nothing to show for it but a cult of selfishness."[2]

The challenge, as L'Engle puts it, is to "turn ourselves off and listen to the story."

> We like to think that "the story" is ours to write, and we attempt to advance the plot according to what we think we deserve. The challenge, as L'Engle puts it, is to "turn ourselves off and listen to the story."

At many critical junctures throughout the history of God's saving activity, he puts an emphasis on remembering. He calls upon his people to summon their collective memory and recount his saving acts.

At the end of Moses' life, when the Israelites stood poised to enter the Promised Land, their leader exhorted them: "Remember the days of long ago; think about the generations past. Ask your father and he will inform you. Inquire of your elders, and they will tell you" (Deuteronomy 32:7). And later, after Moses died, his successor, Joshua, called the tribes together before leading the campaign to take the land and told them: "Remember what Moses, the servant of the Lord, commanded you: 'The LORD your God is giving you rest and has given you this land'" (Joshua 1:13).

Conversely, God's spokespeople have issued prophetic warnings about the consequences of *forgetting* his mighty acts. "They traded their glorious God for a statue of a grass-eating ox! They forgot God, their savior, who had done such great things in Egypt," writes the psalmist (106:20-21). The author of the book of Ecclesiastes laments, "We don't remember what happened in those former times. And in future generations, no one will remember what we are doing now" (Eccles 1:11). He says, "Don't let the excitement of youth cause you to forget your Creator" (Eccles 12:1).

"Remember what happened to Lot's wife!" Jesus warned while explaining the cost of following him (Luke 17:32). And when he established the new covenant in his blood, Jesus commanded his followers to reenact the ritual of communion "in remembrance" of him (Luke 22:19).

Keeping alive the collective memory of God's covenant people is a way of keeping the Story in their minds and hearts. This is all the more critical for the believing community today, when the Grand Narrative threatens to be overtaken by a zillion individual consumer narratives. Keeping alive the memory of God's saving acts will enable our young people to see the scope of God's activity and to find their place in his Story.

In the church models I highlighted and in the forum on the church, teens and their pastors offered helpful insights and inspiring models for how the church can capture the imaginations and allegiance of this generation. But I have said little about what parents can do.

"What good fortune it is to receive a good, truly Christian upbringing, to enter with it into the years of youth," writes the nineteenth-century Russian mystic Theophan the Recluse. "An immaculate youth is a pure sacrifice. This is accomplished by means of overcoming quite a few obstacles.

"A Christian," he continues, "is meant to be a container of extraordinarily exalted powers which are ready to be poured out upon him from the source of all good things, if only he will not put himself into disorder."[3] Parents can go a long way in overcoming some of the "obstacles" and eliminating much of the "disorder" that clutters the minds and souls of young people. Limiting the number of television sets in the home, taking them out of kids' bedrooms or turning off the TV altogether are some ways to diminish this disorder. Peace and quiescence quickly become comfortable companions, and soon indispensable friends.

But diminishing electronic clutter is only part of the picture. Baby boomers are well-known for their abandonment of organized religion during their revolution years. So many have matured into adulthood without religious and biblical moorings and have raised their children in a religious vacuum. Both parents *and* offspring need to be brought back into the Story.

Last Lenten season my sons and I adopted a helpful tool. I put together notebooks for my sons based on Luther's Small Catechism that required them to read the catechism aloud with me and then to answer additional pertinent questions that I put to them on the teachings. For example, the catechism opens with a recitation of the Ten Commandments. In our lesson on the eighth commandment, "You shall not bear false witness against your neighbor," Luther asks, "What does this mean?"

He then provides the answer.

"We should fear and love God, and so we should not tell lies about our neighbor, nor betray, slander, or defame him, but should apologize for him, speak well of him, and interpret charitably all that he does."[4]

My sons and I read these portions of the catechism together out loud, and then I sent them off to write in their notebooks. Pertaining to this commandment, one of the questions I asked was, "Have you violated this commandment by telling lies or betraying or slandering a friend?"

One of my sons answered, "Gossiping about nerds or dorks. I am to love them too."

Later in the catechism Luther addresses the Apostles' Creed, the first part of which reads: "I believe in God, the Father almighty, maker of heaven and earth."

"What does this mean?" Luther asks.

"Answer: I believe that God has created me and all that exists; that he has given me and still sustains my body and soul, all my limbs and senses, my reason and all the faculties of my mind, together with food and clothing, house and home, family and property; that he provides me daily and abundantly with all the necessities of life, protects me from all danger, and preserves me from all evil. All this he does out of his pure, fatherly, and divine goodness and mercy, without any merit or worthiness on my part. For all of this I am bound to thank, praise, serve, and obey him. This is most certainly true."[5]

> I asked, "Have you violated this commandment by telling lies or betraying or slandering a friend?" One of my sons answered, "Gossiping about nerds or dorks. I am to love them too."

My sons and I read aloud these portions of the Creed; they rewrote Luther's answers; and finally, they answered the questions I had attached to each section. For example, pertaining to this portion of the Creed, I asked, "What is your definition of a person's soul?"

One son answered, "The thing that makes the lump of matter alive."

I asked, "How do you feed your soul?"

He answered, "I study things and learn and defeat challenges and learn about God."

> I asked, "What is your definition of a person's soul?" My son answered, "The thing that makes the lump of matter alive."

"Is it possible to starve your soul?"

"Yes, to be bored and sit around all day."

The repetition of saying out loud the commandments, the Creed and later the Lord's Prayer in Luther's catechism stills their edginess and resists their restlessness. The discipline of writing out Luther's answers forces them to settle down, concentrate and think about what they are writing. This contravenes the fast-paced impulses that otherwise drive them. And the question/answer portion that I added gives them the chance to probe more deeply and to apply the historical biblical truths to their individual situations. This places their world into the context of the Grand Narrative. Nerds and dorks become neighbors to be "interpreted charitably." Boredom and laziness begin to be seen as symptoms of starvation of the soul.

In the same way, the approaches to church and youth ministry that I have highlighted are capturing the hearts of churched and unchurched young people because they break through the consumer narratives and show them the Big Story. These models, in various ways, *require something,* make demands and remove the holy from the realm of consumer choices. They penetrate the effects of the electronic haze by countering passivity with interactivity, the lulling of the senses with tactile expressions of worship, isolation with intimacy, distorted worldviews with a view toward eternity.

The interactive prayer, the testimonies and the act of getting up out of the pew to receive Communion at our church forum, like the "ministry time" at Souled Out, require active resolve and a willingness to leave one's comfort zone.

The mentoring models and accountability groups at Shadow Mountain and the confessional prayer in the church forum both create relationships of intimacy and accountability.

The great weight the teens placed on the Lord's Supper, the healing power of hugging and praying for each other during "ministry time" at Souled Out, and "the practices" at Arbutus United Methodist Church reawaken the tactile pleasure of tasting and seeing that the Lord is good.

If God is God, then he is not a consumer option. To know him, love him and serve him defies the "you deserve it all" mindset. Active worship overcomes passive entertainment; intimacy breaks through isolation; the bread and the wine heal the senses and rehabilitate the soul. The *I* in "I'm worth it" is exchanged for the *Thou* in "Thou art worthy."

Worship connects the soul to its source and thereby places it in the Story. "We're in a *story* in which everything eventually comes together," writes Peterson, "a narrative in which all the puzzling parts finally fit. . . . But being in a story means that we mustn't attempt to get ahead of the plot—skip the hard parts, erase the painful parts, detour the disappointments."[6]

"We are invited into becoming full participants in the story of Jesus and shown how to become such

> If God is God, then he is not a consumer option. To know him, love him and serve him defies the "you deserve it all" mindset.

participants," Peterson concludes. "We are not simply *told* that Jesus is the Son of God; we not only *become* beneficiaries of his atonement; we are invited to die his death and live his life with the freedom and dignity of participants. And here is the marvelous thing: we enter the center of the story *without becoming the center* of the story."[7]

So when the plot is surrendered to the rightful author, the "great reversal" is reversed. The bigness-smallness ratio reverts to where it belongs: God writing the script and his creatures joyfully participating in *his* story. Consumers no longer look at what the world can do for them; instead they become disci-

> "We are invited into becoming full participants in the story of Jesus and shown how to become such participants."—
> EUGENE PETERSON

ples, surrendering all rights of ownership of life to serve the greater purpose. When consumers become the disciples, then they will become what Theophan the Recluse says they were created to become: "a container of extraordinary and exalted powers."

I Remember

Miracle though it may have been, my father's deliverance from alcoholism was not the miracle my grandmother had been praying for. Button did not live to see that miracle come true. She died in 1988 as my father was only just finding his way back to the simple faith she had instilled in him during his childhood. Shortly before my father died, a few years after Button's death, he told us of a vision he had of heaven. He said, "All the promises of Jesus are true. There are no empty promises."

So now I cast my son off the cliff of his childhood. And I shudder. I am standing on the edge of the second millennium looking out over the landscape of the third. It is a scary place to be. But I turn and look behind me and see the mountain my father and I climbed during my youth, and the mountain my grandmother climbed with him during his.

I remember their stories. I remember my story. I remember the Story that subsumes them all. There are no empty promises.

"I will teach you hidden lessons from our past—stories we have heard and know, stories our ancestors handed down to us," says the psalmist. "We will not hide these truths from our children but will tell the next generation about the glorious deeds of the LORD" (Psalm 78:2-4). In a letter my father left to the family to read after his death he wrote: "I want to leave this note of comfort for you because I want you to know that I will see face to face my friend Jesus and get an explanation as to how I found my way."

All generations through all ages have "found their way." This one will too. For all the disturbing and crushing aspects of what our young people confront in today's culture, the Millennial generation remains only the latest chapter in the unfolding plot of God's Story. We who precede them must help them turn the page. So as the psalmist also says, "Each generation can set its hope anew on God remembering his glorious miracles" (Psalm 78:7).

Key Points
☐ Consumerism has trained us and our young people to think that our individual stories are ours to write.

☐ For a society like ours where self-fulfillment reigns supreme, there is little evidence that people are truly happy.

☐ When we recall God's saving activity in the biblical record, the historical record and the lives of others, we begin to see his activity in our lives too.

☐ True worship transforms the lulling effects of the media culture.

☐ When we subsume our individual narratives under the sovereignty of God's Story, the appetites of this world are exchanged for hope in the promises of God. The consumer becomes the disciple.

☐ My father told me before he died that all of the promises of Jesus are true. There are no empty promises.

Prayer Point
Make me part of your Story, Lord.

Notes

Chapter 1: The Stakes

[1]Susan Littwin, *The Postponed Generation* (New York: William Morrow, 1986), p. 19. The author gives only the year, 1965, for the issue of *Newsweek* she is citing.

[2]Ibid., p. 22.

[3]Diana West, "Treat Your Children Well," *Wall Street Journal,* April 22, 1998, section A, p. 20.

[4]Evan Thomas, "Hooray for Hypocrisy," *Newsweek,* January 9, 1996, p. 61.

[5]Randall Sullivan, "Lynching in Malibu," *Rolling Stone,* September 4, 1997, p. 58.

[6]Ibid.

[7]*New York,* April 6, 1998, p. 54.

[8]David Denby, "Buried Alive," *New Yorker,* July 15, 1996, p. 56.

[9]The Smashing Pumpkins, "Tales of a Scorched Earth," *Mellon Collie and the Infinite Sadness,* chrysalis songs/cinderful music, 1995.

Chapter 2: Who Are These People?

[1]*New York Times,* April 29, 1998, section D.

[2]Ibid., p. D1.

[3]Taken from Wendy Murray Zoba, "The Class of '00," *Christianity Today,* February 3, 1997, p. 20, for which I gathered these observations from telephone interviews and other resources.

[4]Sydney Lewis, *A Totally Alien Life Form—Teenagers* (New York: New Press, 1996), p. 61.

[5]Culled from questionnaires and teens' quotes I accumulated during my research for Zoba, "Class of '00," and for this book.

[6]William Strauss and Neil Howe, *Generations* (New York: William Morrow, 1991). For the purposes of my book, only the most recent generations apply.

[7]The parameters that define who falls into what generation, in terms of birth year, are fuzzy. For the sake of simplicity, I recognize these dates as "broad strokes." I have exchanged Strauss and Howe's term "Thirteenth Gen" for the more commonly recognized "Generation X," referring to those born between 1965 and 1976. A boomer is a boomer by anyone's definition, and so the designation is retained for those born between 1946 and 1964. My use of these designations is not meant to suggest that I subscribe to the assertions or embrace all of the

conclusions in Strauss and Howe's book. Nor do I mean to imply that social forces predestine these generations to a certain course outside the sovereignty of God. Furthermore, my use of these terms is not intended to suggest that individuals who fall into one of these categories are powerless and at the mercy of their times. These categories serve only to help shape the narrative and enable the reader to apprehend a sense of flow and transition between generations.

[8]The teens' thoughts about the church are discussed in chapter six.

Chapter 3: The Power of the Plug

[1]Craig Kennet Miller, *PostModerns* (Nashville: Discipleship Resources, 1996), pp. 50-51.

[2]Ibid.

[3]Wade Clark Roof, *A Generation of Seekers* (New York: HarperCollins, 1993), p. 42.

[4]"At War with War," *Time,* May 18, 1970 (taken from CD-ROM).

[5]Roof, *Generation of Seekers,* p. 53.

[6]Ibid., p. 54.

[7]Diana West, "Treat Your Children Well," *Wall Street Journal,* April 22, 1998, p. 20.

[8]William Strauss and Neil Howe, *Generations* (New York: William Morrow, 1991) p. 321.

[9]Ibid., pp. 324-26.

[10]Margot Hornblower, "Great Xpectations," *Time,* June 9, 1997, p. 60.

[11]John W. Whitehead, "Losing a Generation to Despair," *Rutherford,* February 1996, p. 13.

[12]Hornblower, "Great Xpectations," p. 60. This downsizing occurred between 1979 and 1995.

[13]Joshua Wolf Shenk, "In Debt All the Way Up to Their Nose Rings," *U.S. News & World Report,* June 9, 1997, p. 38.

[14]Joshua Cooper Ramo, "Peace Is an Xcellent Adventure," *Time,* June 9, 1997, p. 69.

[15]Shenk, "Debt," p. 38.

[16]Ibid.

[17]Ibid., p. 39.

[18]Hornblower, "Great Xpectations," p. 60.

[19]Nancy Hass, "A TV Generation Is Seeing Beyond Color," *New York Times,* February 22, 1998, section 2, p. 1.

[20]Ginia Bellafonte, "Bewitching Teen Heroines," *Time,* May 5, 1997, p. 84.

[21]Barbara DaFoe Whitehead, "Dan Quayle Was Right," *Atlantic Monthly,* April 1993.

[22]Laura Shapiro, "The Myth of Quality Time," *Newsweek,* May 12, 1997.

[23]In a telephone interview, fall 1996.

[24]David Denby, "Buried Alive," *New Yorker,* July 15, 1996, p. 51.

[25]David Wild, "South Park's Evil Geniuses and the Triumph of No-Brow Culture,"

Rolling Stone, February 19, 1998, p. 36.

[26]Letter to the editor, *Newsweek,* April 13, 1998, p. 18.

[27]Rick Marin, "The Rude Tube," *Newsweek,* March 23, 1998, pp. 58-59.

[28]Mike Darnell, "Hot T.V.," *Rolling Stone,* August 21, 1997, p. 69.

[29]Denby, "Buried," p. 48.

[30]Cited in Wendy Murray Zoba, "The Class of '00," *Christianity Today,* February 3, 1997.

[31]"Teenagers and Technology," *Newsweek,* April 28, 1997, p. 86. The poll was taken in cooperation with Princeton Survey Research Associates in March 1997.

[32]Susan Gregory Thomas, "Mini Computer Moguls," *U.S. News & World Report,* May 19, 1997, p. 48.

[33]Ibid.

[34]Lewis Lapham, "In the Garden of Tabloid Delight," *Harper's,* August 1997, p. 39.

[35]Denby, "Buried," p. 50.

[36]Joshua Quittner, "Future Shocks," *Time,* June 8, 1998, pp. 212-13.

[37]Miller, *PostModerns,* p. 160.

[38]Karen Schoemer, "Rockers, Models and the Allure of Heroin," *Newsweek,* August 26, 1996, p. 53.

[39]Ibid.

[40]John Leland, "The Fear of Heroin Is Shooting Up," *Newsweek,* August 26, 1996, p. 55.

[41]Schoemer, "Rockers, Models," p. 51.

[42]Denby, "Buried," pp. 51, 48.

[43]Ibid., p. 51.

Chapter 4: What We Didn't Anticipate

[1]Braven Smillie, "TV Cartoon Gives Japanese Youth Fits," *Washington Times,* December 18, 1997, p. A15.

[2]Ibid.

[3]Ibid.

[4]Andrew Solomon, "Bill Viola's Video Arcade," *New York Times Magazine,* February 8, 1998, p. 34.

[5]Ibid.

[6]Jack Harwell, " 'Bowling Alone,' 'Refrigerator Rights,' and New Churches," *Religion News Service,* February 2, 1998, p. 3.

[7]James Gleick, "Addicted to Speed," *New York Times Magazine,* September 28, 1997, p. 61.

[8]Ibid., p. 54.

[9]Ibid., p. 58.

[10]James Gorman, "The Intimate Reach of Remote Control," *New York Times Magazine,* September 28, 1997, p. 64.

[11]Mark Dery, "The Cult of the Mind," *New York Times Magazine,* September 28,

1997, p. 94.

[12]This was posited by Michael Medved in his plenary session at the 1998 Evangelical Press Association convention, Chicago, April 27, 1998.

[13]Sydney Lewis, *A Totally Alien Life Form—Teenagers* (New York: NewPress, 1996), p. 43.

[14]For the past thirty-one years.

[15]Rene Sanchez, "Singing the Blahs," *Washington Post* national weekly edition, January 19, 1998, p. 34. The study also showed that a record number of college freshmen (26 percent) come from homes where their parents are either divorced or separated and that the number of freshmen who smoke was at its highest level since the surveys began (16 percent, doubling since the 1980s). Drinking habits are improving (53 percent said they drank beer frequently or occasionally, which is down from 72 percent in 1981), but more freshmen believe that marijuana should be legalized (35 percent, which is twice as many as in 1989).

[16]Tom Ehrich, "When Entertainment Rules the Cultural Landscape," *Religion News Service,* January 20, 1998, p. 7.

[17]Mark Edmundson, "On the Uses of a Liberal Education," *Harper's,* September 1997, p. 40.

[18]Taken from the transcript of a question-and-answer session held in my home in November 1998.

[19]Ibid.

[20]Lewis, *Totally Alien Life Form,* p. 87.

[21]Ron Stodhill II, "Where'd You Learn That?" *Time,* June 15, 1998, p. 52.

[22]Todd Gitlin, "Pop Goes the Culture," *U.S. News & World Report,* June 1, 1998, p. 16.

[23]Peter Applebome, "No Room for Children in a World of Little Adults," *New York Times,* May 10, 1998, Sect. 4, p. 1.

[24]Ibid., p. 3.

[25]Ibid.

[26]Bruce Orwall, "Cut the Cute Stuff: Kids Flock to Adult Flicks," *Wall Street Journal,* August 29, 1997, p. B6.

[27]Applebome, "No Room," p. 3.

[28]Richard Lacayo, "Toward the Root of the Evil," *Time,* April 6, 1998, p. 38.

[29]Edmundson, "On the Uses," p. 41.

[30]Lewis Lapham, "In the Garden of Tabloid Delight," *Harpers,* August 1997, pp. 42-43.

[31]Eugene Peterson, *Subversive Spirituality* (Grand Rapids, Mich.: Eerdmans, 1997), p. 6.

[32]Ibid., p. 13.

[33]Joshua Quittner, "Life and Death on the Web," *Time,* April 7, 1997, p. 47.

[34]Erica Goode, "The Eternal Quest for a New Age," *U.S. News & World Report,* April 7, 1997, p. 32.

[35]Michael Novak, "The Most Religious Century," *New York Times,* May 24, 1998,

sect. 4, p. 11.

[36]George H. Gallup, "Is a New Awakening at Hand?" *Emerging Trends* (Princeton Religion Research Center) 18, no. 9 (1996): 1.

[37]"Teens Ponder Meaningful Questions," *Emerging Trends* (Princeton Religion Research Center) 18, no. 9 (1996): 4.

[38]Peterson, *Subversive,* p. 14.

Chapter 5: What Hath Bob Dole to Do with South Park?

[1]Telephone interview, fall 1996.

[2]Ibid.

[3]Andrew Ferguson, "Now They Want Your Kids," *Time,* September 29, 1997, p. 64.

[4]Telephone interview, fall 1996.

[5]Ibid.

[6]Ben Gose, "More Freshmen Than Ever Appear Disengaged," *Chronicle of Higher Education,* January 16, 1998, p. A37. It is also necessary to note that the number of freshmen who said it was important to take personal steps to clean up the environment or promote racial understanding declined. Strangely, the percentage of college freshmen who said marijuana should be legalized—35 percent—was twice as high as it was in 1989.

[7]"Teen-Sex Rate Drops for the First Time in 25 Years," *Religion News Service,* May 1, 1997, p. 3.

[8]Erica Werner, "The Cult of Virginity," *Ms.,* March-April 1997, p. 42.

[9]Kristen Campbell, "Despite Some Negative Images, Teens Quietly Go About Doing Good," *Religion News Service,* March 31, 1997, p. 6.

[10]Christopher John Farley, "Kids and Race," *Time,* November 24, 1997, p. 88.

[11]Ibid.

[12]David B. Wolfe, "The Psychological Center of Gravity," *American Demographics,* April 1998, p. 17.

[13]Ibid., p. 16.

[14]Ibid., p. 17.

[15]Taken from an informal survey I took of a group of approximately one hundred teens, ages thirteen to eighteen, June 1997.

[16]Telephone interview, fall 1996.

[17]Liz Kelly, "Choir Girl," *CCM,* November 1998, p. 28.

[18]Quoted in Wendy Murray Zoba, "The Class of '00," *Christianity Today,* February 3, 1997, p. 24, on the basis of a telephone interview, fall 1996.

[19]Telephone interview, fall 1996.

[20]I conducted telephone interviews with both Ed and Cathi in the fall of 1996.

[21]Telephone interview, fall 1996.

[22]Telephone interview, fall 1996. The Joneses no longer serve at Arbutus United Methodist Church. I am addressing the program that they conceived and implemented during their tenure there.

[23]Telephone interview, fall 1996.
[24]Ibid.
[25]Ibid.
[26]Ibid.

Chapter 6: Does God Have a Face?

[1]From the song "One of Us," written by Eric Bazilian and performed by Joan Osborne, on the album *relish,* PolyGram Records, 1995.

Chapter 7: The Grand Narrative

[1]DeeDee Risher, "Listening to the Story," *The Other Side,* March-April 1998, p. 38.
[2]Eugene Peterson, *Leap over a Wall* (San Francisco: HarperSanFrancisco, 1997), p. 111.
[3]Theophan the Recluse, *Raising Them Right* (Ben Lomond, Calif.: Conciliar, 1989), p. 67.
[4]John H. Leith, ed., *Creeds of the Churches* (Atlanta: John Knox, 1973), p. 114.
[5]Ibid., p. 115.
[6]Peterson, *Leap,* p. 121.
[5]Eugene Peterson, *Subversive Spirituality* (Grand Rapids, Mich.: Eerdmans, 1997), p. 15. I am weaving together Peterson's thoughts from two sources, both of which advance the "Story" theme.